London Borough of Hounslow

Hounslow Library Services

This item should be returned or renewed by the latest date shown. If it is not required by another reader, you may renew it in person or by telephone (twice only). Please quote your library card number. A charge will be made for items returned or renewed after the date due.

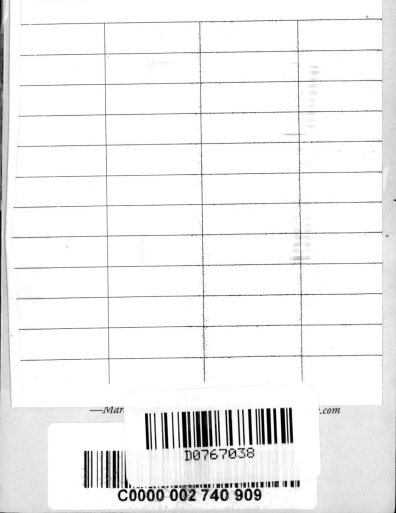

The
SOUL
of
LEADERSHIP

Unlocking Your Potential for Greatness

DEEPAK CHOPRA

RIDER

LONDON • SYDNEY • AUCKLAND • JOHANNESBURG

3 5 7 9 10 8 6 4 2

This edition published 2011 by Rider, an imprint of Ebury Publishing
A Random House Group company
First published in the United States of America by Harmony Books in 2010

Copyright © 2010 Deepak Chopra

The Random House Group Limited Reg. No. 954009

Addresses for companies within the Random House Group can be found at
www.randomhouse.co.uk

A CIP catalogue record for this book is available from the British Library

The Random House Group Limited supports The Forest Stewardship Council
(FSC), the leading international forest certification organisation. All our titles
that are printed on Greenpeace approved FSC certified paper carry the FSC
logo. Our paper procurement policy can be found at
www.rbooks.co.uk/environment

Mixed Sources
Product group from well-managed
forests and other controlled sources
www.fsc.org Cert no. TT-COC-2139
© 1996 Forest Stewardship Council
FSC

Printed and bound in Great Britain by Clays Ltd, St Ives plc

ISBN 9781846044939

To buy books by your favourite authors and register for offers visit
www.rbooks.co.uk

Contents

INTRODUCTION

Becoming a leader is the most crucial choice one can make—it is the decision to step out of darkness into the light.

We have never needed enlightened leadership as much as we do now. Surely this refrain has been heard throughout the ages, but in the second decade of the twenty-first century, humankind poses a terrible threat to its own existence as we blindly tear great holes in the life-sustaining fabric of our environment. We can no longer turn to government, however well meaning it may be, or to anyone beyond ourselves, to provide answers for the great problems of our time. And even in turning to ourselves we must go beyond the constant clamor of ego, beyond the tools of logic and reason, to the still, calm place within us: the realm of the soul.

Here we can begin by asking the basic questions that give our lives meaning. Who am I? Why am I here? How can I tune in the soft-spoken urgings of the soul to fulfill my life's purpose and to make a difference? In answering these questions to the best of our ability, each of us must step into the role of leader, taking responsibility first for directing our own lives, and then for interacting with other people—at work, at home, and everywhere in between. As we continue to draw on the soul for direction, we will eventually find that other people are turning to us for guidance, drawn to us by our ability to treat them with dignity and to skillfully respond to their needs from a higher place.

My aim in this book is to give everyone the skills and insights to be a leader—not just any leader but an inspired one. At the deepest level, a leader is the symbolic soul of the group. His role is to fulfill the needs of others and, when each need is met, to lead the group on to fulfill ever higher needs, lifting the group's potential at every step. The inspired leader's power base comes not from other people but from her very being, and the path she walks is guided by her own soul. Its hallmarks are creativity, intelligence, organizing power, and love.

Everyone who has a soul, which by my definition includes us all, has the potential to be an inspired leader. When you change on the inside so that you draw on the unlimited wisdom of the soul, you become a leader without needing to seek followers. As you put your vision for a better world into tangible form, they will find you. It is my fondest hope that after reading these pages, countless readers like you will discover their greatness and act upon it. Of these leaders, untold numbers may become public figures, and even more will perform a leadership role at work, at home, and in the community. Wherever you do it, there is no doubt in my mind that leading from the soul is what the time demands.

As you'll see in the pages that lie ahead, the leadership I'm talking about in this book is not leadership as we've traditionally defined it. According to that old definition, leadership belongs to the few. In a group the person selected to lead may stand out as the most popular, confident, or ruthless. By these measures, not everyone can lead. When the strong and ruthless rise on the world stage, we find ourselves led by kings and generals, autocrats and dictators, power-hungry premiers and presidents. History traffics in myth making, which is based on personal charisma and uses spin to evoke an aura of destiny. But these measures of leadership are flawed. None of the qualities mentioned here indicate that a leader will actually improve the lives of those who follow him. Chances are equally good that such leadership will bring misery, conflict, and oppression. The old definitions of leadership exalt power, and the use of power has always been directly linked to its abuse.

Because leaders have turned out to be so completely unpredictable, and because so few great leaders have emerged from the ranks of those who have seized power, we have been led to believe that perhaps there is some invisible hand at work, selecting which leader will be great. But this is only more spin. The criteria for inspired leadership don't need to be shadowed in mystery. In fact, they are simple: great leaders are those who can respond to their own needs and the needs of others from the higher levels of spirit with vision, creativity, and a sense of unity with the people they lead.

You can be such a leader. The path is open to you. The only requirement is that you listen to your own inner guide. Once you step onto this path, you are on your way to becoming what I call a *successful visionary*. A successful visionary makes his or her vision manifest in the world. Invisible seeds planted in the silence of your deepest awareness become tangible, visible realities. As they unfold, you will manage their growth with passion and energy. Your purpose will be apparent to all. The results you achieve will benefit everyone—you, the group you lead, and the world at large. On a planet challenged on every side with ecological deterioration, everything you achieve must be sustainable, which means supported by awareness. This is an essential part of any vision of the future that draws on the soul.

When I talk about the soul, I'm not referring to the soul as defined by any particular religion, although all the great spiritual traditions acknowledge its existence. I believe the soul is an expression of an underlying universal field of consciousness. Your particular awareness, or soul, is like a wave in this boundless sea, unique for a brief moment in time before it falls back into the larger entity from which it emerged. At the soul level you are seamlessly connected with everything in the universe, to the silent domain from which all matter and energy spring.

In this context it is not surprising that the soul takes on qualities that are essential to creation: creativity, intelligence, organizing power, and love. If you find this notion difficult to accept, perhaps you'll agree with me that the old way of living on this planet is reaching its limits, and that the time has come to try something new. If you find that, by turning to the soul for leadership in the ways I describe in this book, you are able to increase the creativity, intelligence, organizing power, and love in your life and in your larger world, you can choose to credit your soul or not. It won't care, and those who share the world with you will be grateful, regardless of what terms you use to describe your new way of being.

A MAP FOR THE ROAD AHEAD

Leadership is an evolving journey. The twists and turns lying before you are unpredictable. But you can be provided with a map. The text that follows divides the map into three parts.

First, I have laid out the core of what it means to lead from the soul in a convenient acronym, L-E-A-D-E-R-S, with each letter outlining a key aspect of defining your vision and then bringing it to fruition.

L = Look and listen. Do this with your senses, as an unbiased observer who has not judged anything in advance. Do it with your heart, obeying your truest feelings. Finally, do it with your soul, responding to the vision and deep purpose it provides.

E = Emotional bonding. Leading from the soul means going beyond the melodrama of living in crisis mode. It requires recognizing and clearing away toxic emotions so you can clearly understand your own specific needs, and those of others.

A = Awareness. This means being aware of the questions that underlie every challenge: Who am I? What do I want? What does the situation demand? A leader must continually ask these questions of herself, and inspire her team to ask them for themselves.

D = Doing. A leader must be action-oriented. In whatever he does, he must serve as a role model, holding himself responsible for the promises he has made. This requires persistence and tenacity, but also the ability to view any situation with flexibility and humor.

E = Empowerment. The soul's power comes from self-awareness that is responsive to feedback but independent of the good or bad opinion of others. Empowerment isn't selfish. It raises the status of leader and team together.

R = Responsibility. Responsible leadership includes choosing considered risks rather than reckless ones, walking the talk, having integrity, and living up to your inner values. Seen from the level of the soul, a leader's greatest responsibility is to lead the group on the path of higher consciousness.

S = *Synchronicity.* This is a mysterious element from the underlying universal field of consciousness that all great leaders harness. Synchronicity is the ability to create good luck and find invisible support that carries one beyond predicted outcomes to a higher plane. In spiritual terms, synchronicity is the ultimate ability to connect any need with an answer from the soul.

The map of leadership comes into more specific focus in the second part of this book, through the stories of ordinary people who have become successful visionaries. Here we'll follow two such people—Jeremy Moon and Renata M. Black—who began with no material means and went on to lead successful multimillion-dollar enterprises that make a difference in the world. In both cases the vision that started their journey was fueled with passion and purpose. That's not unusual in success stories, but here we also find deeper values, drawn from the realm of soul.

As we'll see, Jeremy's and Renata's paths followed the steps described in the acronym L-E-A-D-E-R-S; everything from looking and listening to synchronicity played a crucial role. Besides being inspiring, this part of the book will give you more confidence that leading from the soul is a viable choice in the rough-and-tumble of the real world. In fact, by choosing visionary leadership as a path to success, the real world became a miraculous place for both leaders, a place where material success took a backseat to personal discovery.

The third part of the book is a brief summary of what you will have learned. I hope it is couched in such a way as to make it easier for you to recognize the landmarks of soulful leadership as they begin to make themselves known in your life.

WHY THE SOUL?

How do leaders emerge from ordinary lives? Every group naturally gives rise to leaders who guide it to a shared goal. Yet some leaders fail, while others succeed. Some are destroyed by a flawed strategy, or by the overwhelming stress of their role. And when crisis arises, leaving us crying out for great leaders, there is a constant threat that such a figure will not appear, leaving the infamous "leadership vacuum" that has become such a chronic problem in our modern society.

In the deeper reality of the soul, a family in disarray, a company without vision, or a nation struggling to adopt a new level of freedom needs to respond to hidden spiritual drives and needs. Once this is understood, countless leaders can rise to the highest levels of greatness. Inspired leadership is established in being, where there is no need to adopt a strategy for climbing to the top. As you unfold your potential for greatness, you unfold the same potential in others. They will naturally turn to you for guidance and leadership in the way forward, and one day they themselves will be able to provide enlightened leadership to others.

Our souls offer the highest inspiration at every moment. With our minds we may see chaos, but the soul knows there is an underlying order, and seeks to find it.

Until we turn to the quiet wisdom of the soul, we will continue to fall back on old habits and stale answers in response to new challenges. We will stay mired in pointless struggles and confusion. But when we do understand the ways of the soul, and draw on them, someone will emerge to cut through the fog. Mahatma Gandhi, Mother Teresa, and Nelson Mandela undertook their journeys based on the soul's awareness (however much we clothe them in mythic status). They used this awareness to tap into a source of wisdom that remains constant throughout history and is available to us all.

In any group the members are acting out two basic themes in life—need and response. If we could see ourselves clearly, each of us would realize every day that:

• There is something we need, ranging from the basic need for food and shelter to the higher needs of self-worth, love, and spiritual meaning;

• There is some response that will fill that need, ranging from struggle and competition to creative discovery and divine inspiration.

These two themes dominate our inner and outer lives. They override all other forces, and like the workings of the soul they are not random. Needs and responses can be organized in a natural order. Lower needs and responses are followed by higher ones. (As the German writer Bertolt Brecht declared, "Don't talk to me of my soul until you've filled my stomach.") This rising scale is known as *the hierarchy of needs*. As a leader, if you are aware of the hierarchy of needs and their responses, you will be able to continue to respond effectively as the group's needs move up the scale from basic to increasingly spiritual. This is the most powerful thing a leader can do.

For example, extreme social movements (fascism, religious fundamentalism, ethnic nationalism, etc.) draw upon fear, the most primitive response of a group, which matches its most primitive need: survival. External pressures such as economic depression, social migration, and competitive forces also trigger this need. Vaclav Havel was a Czech poet who became president of the new republic after the fall of Communism because he fulfilled his countrymen's basic need for safety, and then went on to address their higher needs for unity and self-worth, which had been suppressed for decades. Dr. Martin Luther King, Jr., offered an oppressed minority the opportunity to go beyond the need to survive in order to meet their higher needs for a sense of dignity and spiritual purpose. He offered transformation. Buddha and Christ offered their followers an opportunity to meet their needs at the highest level, the universal desire for unity.

Through the example of these great leaders, we see that leading from the soul is neither mysterious nor abstract. Inspired leadership matches real responses to real needs. This is a skill that can be learned. You can do it, and so can I. We can meet needs at every level of a group's outer and inner life, applying the same awareness to a family, or a community, as to a corporation. In the deeper reality of the soul, leaders and followers co-create each other. They form an invisible spiritual bond. Leaders exist to embody the values that followers hunger for, while followers fuel the leader's vision from inside themselves.

THE BASIC PRINCIPLES

The journey that a leader takes is one of expanding awareness. The soul itself has complete awareness; it perceives every aspect of a situation. Its perspective is available to you, but ordinarily you don't access it because of your own inner obstacles. We see what we want to see—or what our biases and limitations encourage us to see. On your journey to inspired leadership you will learn how to remove these obstacles. When you do, what was once difficult will become effortless, as your soul clears the way for you. Your vision becomes clearer, and so does the path ahead, until it seems that the universe itself is conspiring to provide the creativity, intelligence, organizing power, and love that lie at the heart of visionary leadership.

PART ONE

L-E-A-D-E-R-S

One

L = LOOK AND LISTEN

Great leaders have a vision, and the ability to manifest it. Defining your own vision begins with looking and listening. You look and listen to the situation around you, but you also look and listen inside. Four steps are involved:

> *Impartial observation—Look and listen with your senses.*
> *Analysis—Look and listen with your mind.*
> *Feeling—Look and listen with your heart.*
> *Incubation—Look and listen with your soul.*

Once you have gone through these four steps, your personal vision can begin to express itself.

The best qualities you can have when starting your career are passion, core values, and dedication to a purpose. These are the elements from which a vision is forged. When you talk to the most inspiring leaders, the kind I call successful visionaries, it turns out that they all began with passion and a view of the big picture. They brought dedication to a deeply felt purpose. They held core values that they were not willing to surrender. In order to find greatness in yourself, these elements should be your primary focus.

Over the years, researchers have tried to find external reasons for the rise of successful leaders. Based on this research, it might seem that being born into wealth, going to the best schools, associating with other successful people, and scoring high on IQ tests would more or less guarantee that a person would turn into a leader. But as we all know, you can start with nothing and still emerge as a great leader, whereas you can start off in life with any number of advantages and achieve little or nothing of value. External advantages give anyone a head start, but they are not a guarantee of success.

So what if we reverse this approach and look instead at things that we all possess? Everyone knows how to look and listen—these are the basic tools of perception. But in a leader they grow into something more. A leader is responsible for having a vision, which must be clear enough to guide others and inspire them. Having articulated her vision, a leader must be able to manifest it. The greatest ideas are nothing more than daydreams until they are pushed to become reality. If you want to be a successful visionary, here is where the journey begins, with two crucial questions: What is my vision? How can I make it happen?

No vision is created in a vacuum. It emerges from the situation at hand. That situation can be a crisis or a routine project, a management problem or a financial emergency, anything that requires a leader to offer guidance, to assess the situation by looking and listening at the deepest level possible. This pertains to parents and sports coaches, mentors and counselors, managers and CEOs. Anytime you are called upon to guide, teach, command, motivate, inspire, or plan, opportunity is knocking.

Imagine three people seated on a couch in an outer office, all dressed in their best business attire. The office itself belongs to a venture capitalist who has agreed to give each of them a half hour to present a proposal for a start-up company. Success or failure depends upon this meeting. Who among the three will emerge as a leader, the one with the best chance of persuading the venture capitalist?

The first person feels so nervous his palms are sweaty. He tries to make casual conversation but realizes that he's babbling, so he falls silent. He closes his eyes, reviewing one last time the speech he is going to make. He got very little sleep the night before, having spent hours going over every word of his presentation. He keeps thinking one thing: *Now or never. It's do or die.*

The second person looks much calmer. He's quite confident, in fact. He believes in his idea; he's certain his new business will succeed once he finds a backer. Tall and clear-eyed, he's used to being looked up to. In the back of his mind, he wonders if he can talk the venture capitalist into going out for a round of golf or a pickup basketball game. One-on-one has always been his best mode of persuasion.

The third person is scanning the room with open curiosity. She notices the rich Oriental rug and fresh flowers on the reception desk, but she's more interested in the employees going in and out of the venture capitalist's inner office. They're dressed in jeans and skirts, not suits. They look focused and intent but not stressed. Checking inside herself, the third person feels much the same way. Whatever happens, she's open to the outcome. Once she sets eyes on the venture capitalist, she'll know what kind of personality she's dealing with and respond accordingly.

Of these three people, the first one isn't looking and listening to much beyond his own feelings, which are tense and closed off. The second man is more comfortable and is beginning to see from the heart. He assesses people and situations by how they feel. The third person goes a step further, however. She is entirely open to her surroundings, looking and listening intently. From the clues she picks up, she begins to build a scenario. She can envision herself in the scenario, and as it unfolds, she will adapt. If it turns out that she doesn't fit in, she won't make the mistake of taking the venture capitalist's money; if the compatibility isn't there, she'll move on and find it elsewhere.

In this imaginary scenario we can see that the leader with the greatest potential in this moment is the one who can look and listen from the deepest level. Leadership requires a sound basis inside yourself. When you can arrive at the point where looking and listening comes from your entire being, you are setting the stage to be an inspiring leader.

FOUR LEVELS OF PERCEPTION

To be truly insightful, looking and listening must occur on four different levels. Seeing with our eyes is only the beginning. When we look and listen fully, we involve the body, the mind, the heart, and the soul.

> *Body:* The stage of observing and information gathering
> *Mind:* The stage of analysis and judgment
> *Heart:* The stage of feeling
> *Soul:* The stage of incubation

Once you are satisfied that you have gone through all these stages, your vision in any given moment will emerge as the true expression of who you are, and it will be founded on deep understanding.

Observation: Begin by being as open and impartial as possible. See as much as you can, and listen to whoever has something to say. In a sense you function like a video camera. Allow sights and sounds to come in freely and objectively.

Analysis: At the same time, your mind is also taking in the situation. It begins to weigh and analyze. Allow any and every idea to come to mind. Watch what arises, and notice wisps of answers, new interpretations, and novel combinations. Once again, steer clear of judgments and preconceptions. Be unbiased and clear-headed.

Feeling: At the level of your heart, notice what feels right. Feeling is subtler and truer than pure analysis. This is the level where sudden insight can strike you. You are bringing intuition into the picture, allowing for the "aha" moment that accompanies quantum leaps of creativity.

Incubation: Now let go and wait. When a vision is incubating, it goes into a deep, invisible place. A profound and infinite intelligence nurses your vision, adapting it to your needs and the needs of everyone around you. You have gained access to something greater than yourself, whether you call it the higher self, pure awareness, or your connection with God. If none of these terms work for you, you might want to think of the soul as "who I really am."

A leader, therefore, emerges from within himself. He matches his inner perception with the outer situation. A twenty-four-year-old Indian arriving in South Africa in 1893 saw that he would be beaten if he refused to ride on the running board of a stagecoach to make room for white European passengers. If he insisted on riding in the first-class compartment of a train because he had a first-class ticket, he would be told that his place was in third class, no matter what his ticket said. Yet if that twenty-four-year-old happened to be Mohandas Gandhi, he could evaluate his situation using all four levels of perception. With his eyes he looked around and perceived discrimination. With his heart he felt that the situation was intolerable. With his mind he analyzed that a new tactic—civil disobedience— could change things. With his being he committed himself to a vision of freedom, whatever the price.

Current leadership training, almost anywhere you look for it, uses the word *vision* freely, but most often its basis is intellectual. Potential leaders are taught to use their minds to analyze various hypothetical scenarios. By leaving out feeling, intuition, insight, and the profound wisdom of the soul, this training falls short of its potential. No one can deny the simple truth that the greatest leaders are also great souls. Faced with apartheid in South Africa, slavery before the Civil War, or colonial domination in India, their eyes saw the same thing that everyone else saw. Their minds had the same thoughts as countless others around them. In their hearts they felt the same injustice. But Nelson Mandela, Abraham Lincoln, and Mahatma Gandhi each went deeper and asked, from the core of his being, how to elicit a new response, how to turn a new vision into reality.

FINDING YOUR TRUE PURPOSE

Being in touch with the soul is the secret of great leadership. We are all capable of following the path that unites body, mind, heart, and soul. By making a soul connection, your true purpose in life will become the foundation of everything you do. Leaders exist to give of themselves, and you can give only from what you have. The soul—that is, the core of your true self—is the place where you will locate insight, creativity, imagination, and profound intelligence. When you know what is happening at your very core, what you have to give becomes limitless.

In this chapter you will be formulating your life purpose in a single sentence, and once you are sure that this statement expresses your mission deeply and truly, you will refine it further to a single word. The mission statement of Martin Luther King, Jr., could have been "I am here to end racial discrimination and social injustice." Refined to a single word, it might be "freedom." The mission statement of Charles Darwin could have been "I am here to observe how life changes and adapts to the environment." Refined to a single word, it might be "evolution."

Your mission statement will fuse two components that we will develop in this chapter: a Soul Profile that reflects your values, and a Personal Vision that reflects your deepest intentions.

Your Soul Profile

Using just a few words or phrases, answer the following questions. Be candid, and don't dwell too long on the questions before you answer them. Let your first responses guide you.

1. What's my contribution in life?
2. What's the purpose in what I do?

3. How do I feel when I have a peak experience?
4. Who are my heroes and heroines (from history, mythology, fiction, religion)?
5. What are the qualities that I look for in a best friend?
6. What are my unique skills and talents?
7. What are the best qualities I express in a personal relationship?

Now, using the key words you've developed in your answers above, write a brief profile of your soul as if you were describing another person. For example: "Deepak's purpose is to **grow** personally and to **bring out inner potential** and **hidden possibilities**. He contributes by being **loving** and **supportive**. When he has a peak experience, he feels great **inner peace** and **unity** with everything around him. His heroes are **Gandhi, Buddha, Jesus, Mother Divine, and Krishna**. In a best friend he looks for **understanding** and **stimulation**. He feels that his unique skill is **communication**. He has a talent for **getting others to look beyond their old conditioning and fixed boundaries**. His best quality in personal relationships is to **love, support, and appreciate** the other person."

Keeping your soul profile close at hand, now move on to the next step: defining your personal vision.

Your Personal Vision

Again using just a few words or phrases, complete the following sentences. Let yourself go. Don't worry about being logical, or about the feasibility of implementing these ideas. Just write whatever comes to you. And above all, be true to yourself.

1. I want to live in a world in which _____.
2. I would be inspired to work in an organization that _____.
3. I would be proud to lead a team that _____.
4. A transformed world would be _____.

To match your present work with your vision, answer the following:

• How does your work in the world reflect the vision you outlined above?

• What do you need (from your team or organization) to get closer to your ideals?

• What can you offer (to your team and organization) to move it closer to your ideals?

It may be that your present work is far from what your vision would want it to be. The first step toward bridging that gap is to define your vision as specifically as possible. Vague ideals remain passive; a focused purpose awakens the unseen powers of the soul. On the other hand, you may be well on your way to achieving your vision, or at least you may have made the first steps. There is no right place to be right now. The point here is to clarify what kind of world you envision and how you see yourself in it.

Your Mission Statement

Now that you have written down your values and your vision, merge the two into a succinct statement of your overall mission in this lifetime. Your statement should describe what you want to accomplish as a leader from this point forward. Use the following template:

My mission behind everything I do is _____.

- Keep it simple and concise.
- A child should be able to understand it.
- You should be able to state it even in your sleep.

Example: My own mission statement originally was "to reach critical mass and achieve a peaceful, just, sustainable, and healthy world." This needed to be simplified, which led me to come up with a clearer mission: "To serve the world and all who live in it."

Finally, see if you can crystallize your mission statement into one word. Mine is "serve." Yours might be "grow," "evolve," "inspire," "peace," or anything else. The key is that when you hit upon the most succinct way of stating your purpose, you will be listening to your true self, which is the first requirement for anyone who aspires to lead from the soul.

As a leader, your vision exists to be shared with enthusiasm and inspiration. The word *enthusiasm* comes from the Greek root *en-theos* or "in God," reminding you that you must look in your soul. *Inspiration* comes from the same Latin root as *to breathe* and *spirit*. When you inspire others, you bring everyone into the spirit of your vision—you motivate them to breathe together in the same atmosphere.

PUTTING YOUR VISION TO WORK

A vision is general; situations are specific. In every group situation you are going to find human beings, complete with complex feelings, beliefs, habits, experiences, memories, and agendas. Any leader is in a position to inspire such a group, but it takes a successful visionary to influence every one of those aspects, most of which are hidden and highly personal. So having a vision is only your first step. Now you must know how to enter situations and handle them at every level, from superficial (but necessary) managerial tasks to articulating the core of values and beliefs that each of us protects and cherishes.

Situations that cry out for leadership are easy to find. The next step is to focus on the precise need that will bring productive change. As you begin to assess what is needed, you will soon discover that a need is different from a goal. The goal of a group may be to create a new marketing campaign, set up a production schedule, or reassign work to new management teams; but at a less visible level the leader must fulfill some basic needs that will determine whether the goal is achievable. We have already touched briefly on these needs, which are universal. There are seven of them, listed below in ascending order.

The Needs of the Group

Safety, security
Achievement, success

Cooperation
Nurturing, belonging
Creativity, progress
Moral values
Spiritual fulfillment

The pioneer who came up with this list of what people need and arranged it into this hierarchy was the late psychologist Abraham Maslow. He determined that the most basic need (safety and security) must be met before a person can move on to higher needs (love and social contact, for example). In the context of leadership, we're applying Maslow's hierarchy to groups, which requires some minor adjustments to those needs, but the principle of meeting the most basic needs before moving on to higher ones still holds true.

A leader cannot make the mistake of trying to rise above basic needs before everyone feels those needs have been met. And it takes immersion in the situation—hands-on experience—to read what is going on. People don't wear signs announcing what they need—quite the opposite. The chronic complainer may actually be afraid of losing his job; his need is for security. The outspoken critic of new ideas may feel left out; her need is for nurturing. Although we've been discussing groups at work—project teams, the office you work in, the management group you belong in—these needs are universal, so they apply wherever you go. The group could be your family, a volunteer organization, or a Scout troop. To be the soul of the group, a leader must correctly perceive what everyone needs and then put her perceptions into action.

As a guide, here are some common situations that revolve around the seven needs:

1. Safety, Security

Situations of *threat and instability*. People feel insecure. Discontent is in the air. You can see nervous faces, feel the prevailing anxiety. Who is going to make the situation feel safer?

2. Achievement, Success

Situations of *unrealized achievement*. People feel unsuccessful. They want to be more productive, but there's not enough fire or passion to make it happen. Who is going to step up and provide the motivation so sorely needed?

3. Cooperation

Situations of *incoherence and fragmentation*. There's no team spirit. The group disintegrates into bickering and petty wrangling. Meetings go on forever but reach no conclusion. Who's going to be the glue that brings coherence to the situation?

4. Nurturing, Belonging

Situations mired in *bad feeling and apathy*. Everyone is going through the motions, doing what they need to do, but feeling disengaged. There's little personal support or trust. Who's going to bring heart to the situation and make others feel that they belong?

5. Creativity, Progress

Situations dominated by *old solutions and stale ideas*. People feel stymied. Everyone agrees that something new is needed, but all that emerges are small variations on the status quo. Who's going to bring the spark of creativity to the situation?

6. Moral Values

Situations that are *spiritually empty and corrupt*. The weak feel hopeless, and the strong are cynically taking advantage. People talk about righting wrongs, but no one knows where to start. The future feels like wishful thinking; the present is oppressive and suffocating. Who will bring hope and a renewed sense of innocence?

7. Spiritual Fulfillment

Situations that symbolize *the human condition*. People are asking the big questions: Who am I? Why am I here? Many are seeking God. There is talk of a higher reality, yet faith is lacking. Who can bring the light and demonstrate that holiness is a living reality?

So far we've focused on looking, but listening is vitally important when it comes to understanding the situation you are in, and what need is crying out to be fulfilled. In almost every estimate of what makes a leader, the same quality is mentioned: she's a good listener. There's real skill involved in becoming a good listener. When you meet one, the following factors are present.

WHAT MAKES A GOOD LISTENER?

1. Not interrupting.
2. Showing that you empathize: not criticizing, arguing, or patronizing.
3. Establishing a physical sense of closeness without invading personal space.
4. Observing body language and letting yours show you are not distracted but attentive.
5. Offering your own self-disclosures, but not too many, or too soon.
6. Understanding the context of the other person's life.
7. Listening from all four levels: body, mind, heart, and soul.

As with looking, listening begins with your senses, as you try to take in the other person's story without judgment or partiality. Then you go beyond what you hear to analyze it with your mind. You also feel with your heart what the words are trying to convey—most people are expressing far more on the feeling level than the literal meaning of their words might indicate. Finally, you let the words resonate with your soul, letting them incubate before you offer any advice or take any action.

The hierarchy of need is like a ladder, but life is about people—complex entities in the best of circumstances. Instead of a ladder to climb, life presents us with a ball of yarn to untangle. Situations overlap. Conditions constantly shift. Therefore you must remain flexible, looking and listening in order to draw out the true need you are there to fulfill.

Leadership is a way of life—a way you can now choose. A leader moves with life as naturally as possible even when there is no one following. Every step of the way he carries something with him, and this something sets him apart. It isn't charisma, self-confidence, ambition, or ego. Those qualities are identified with prominent leaders, but none are essential. The essential element is ever-expanding awareness, which begins with looking and listening.

The Lessons of Looking and Listening

- Leading from the soul means looking and listening on four levels: body, mind, heart, and soul.
- Once you have your own vision, it motivates and drives everything you do.
- As a leader, you must respond to the hierarchy of needs, from the most basic to the highest.

WHAT TO DO TODAY

It's time to begin applying your vision to the needs of others. Today look around at the group that matters most to you—a team at work, your family, or a volunteer or school group. What does your group need? What response can you provide? (Focus on what you see today; in later chapters, once the most basic needs have been met, we'll discuss how to lead the group to higher ones.)

Your natural strengths will come out in your response to the situation, so consider from the list below how well a leader's response matches your own:

Need: Safety, security

Leader's response: I'm strong when it comes to defending others. I keep my head in a crisis; I'm good in an emergency.

Need: Achievement, success

Leader's response: I know what it takes to win. I can motivate people to achieve. I can make them believe in me.

Need: Cooperation

Leader's response: I'm a conciliator who can see both sides of a conflict. I'm steady and not impulsive. I know how to get people out of their entrenched positions.

Need: Nurturing, belonging

Leader's response: Empathy comes easily to me. I understand human nature. I know how to get people to forgive and see the best in one another. Handling emotional situations doesn't fluster me; I'm comfortable with it.

Need: Creativity, progress

Leader's response: I can get people to think outside the box. I know what makes creative people tick. I love to explore new possibilities. The unknown doesn't frighten me.

Need: Moral values

Leader's response: I feel a calling. I want to heal old wounds, and I can help people see their higher purpose for being here. I want to share my understanding of why we were put on this earth.

Need: Spiritual fulfillment

Leader's response: I feel whole. I influence others who want the experience of inner peace that I have. My inner silence speaks louder than words. I lead through my presence. Others consider me wise.

The fruit of looking and listening is that you work from your own vision. It is your passion, not because you thought it up, but because it comes from who you really are. When you enter the situation and give of yourself as you really are, you grow along with the people you are helping. This is a merging of hearts, minds, and souls.

Two

E = EMOTIONAL BONDING

Leaders bring out the best in others, but successful visionaries go even further: they form lasting emotional bonds. They are the kinds of leaders we hold in our hearts. When people are emotionally bonded to you, they want to have contact with you. They want to be of service and share in your vision. Deep motivation then develops. True, lasting loyalties are formed.

To create such bonds, you must be willing to build real relationships. Share yourself. Take a personal interest in others, and notice their strengths. At the most basic level, you must display healthy emotional energy yourself. Avoid the three toxic A's: authoritarianism, anger, and aloofness.

In every situation, make it a habit to ask yourself the key questions of emotional intelligence: How do I feel? How do they feel? What are the hidden stumbling blocks between us? A leader who can answer these questions will be in a position to create lasting emotional bonds.

Emotions are the invisible allies of successful visionaries. To carry out your vision, you need to master this next area. When you think of a powerful leader, do you imagine a strong authority figure, a boss who cannot be defied, whose disapproval is to be feared? Traditionally, leaders have sought to exercise authority, control, and power. In the long run this strategy doesn't succeed; when motivated by fear, people perform either reluctantly or not at all. A leader working with positive emotions, however, is able to unfold the potential of everyone under her. If you are truly the soul of the group, you lead and serve at the same time. When others sense that you are willing to give of yourself, your influence as a leader will expand tremendously.

Successful visionaries in all ages forged emotional bonds, often instinctively and without a conscious agenda. We can tell that a bond exists because of the behavior of those around them:

> *They want to be in the leader's presence.*
> *They want to be of service.*
> *They want to perform at their best, which brings*
>   *them closer to the leader.*
> *They want to share in the leader's vision.*
> *They want to participate in the leader's success.*

None of this behavior is slavish; it's how a group functions when it feels inspired. Inspiration begins with emotional commitment. Stop for a moment, and consider a leader who inspires you. If you were offered the opportunity to be close to that person, wouldn't you want to have personal contact, share in her vision, and be fulfilled by her success? These are qualities of emotional bonding.

BECOME EMOTIONALLY INTELLIGENT

Emotional bonding isn't the same as being touchy-feely, overly personal, or wearing your heart on your sleeve. It's about working from a high level of emotional intelligence, which has become an aspect of practical psychology. To be more specific, some basic principles grow out of emotional intelligence, allowing you to be emotionally clear and effective. These are skills that any successful visionary must possess.

Emotional Freedom: In order to bond effectively with others, you must be emotionally free. This means, first of all, being free of guilt, resentment, grievances, anger, and aggression. You aren't required to be perfect, only to be clear about your own underlying feelings. We all have negative emotions, but a leader deals with them effectively, for the good of the group. He doesn't give mixed signals or indulge in outbursts and moods—and if he does, he quickly makes amends. Only in clarity can you trust yourself emotionally and have others trust you.

To reach a point of clarity, it's very useful to:

• Stay aware of your body. Sensations of tightness, constriction, stiffness, discomfort, and pain are indications that negative emotions are asking to be acknowledged and released.

• Witness your feelings. Emotions suck us in and inevitably color our judgment. But if you observe your emotions objectively, as passing events whose influence will diminish over time, you can resist being drawn in by them.

• Express your feelings. This means, first and foremost, expressing them to yourself when you know that they are negative and potentially destructive. Learn how to release your negativity in private, and be diligent about it. Don't let anger and resentment linger just because you have walked away. Unless you actively acknowledge and release them, they will build up and fester.

• Take responsibility for what you feel. When someone else makes a mistake, it is her responsibility to correct it, but it is your responsibility to handle how you feel about it—that emotion doesn't belong to anyone but you. It often helps to keep a journal of your emotional life, both positive and negative. Give yourself credit when you've handled a tough situation without blowing up, blaming, or turning resentful. Take responsibility for the times when your emotions had an adverse effect on your leadership. Journals are good places to be totally honest and admit your flaws, with the aim of improving on them.

• Share your feelings with people you trust. Everyone needs a loved one or close confidant who will listen, understand, and offer a different view.

• Find additional perspectives. Emotions are closely tied to beliefs, ego, and past conditioning. When you get angry at someone, you are also saying, "I'm right." Defuse this self-centered tendency by asking for as many viewpoints as possible. Finding out what others think won't make you wrong; it will broaden your vistas.

Doing these things is not just good for you. When you're emotionally free, it makes other people comfortable and happy to be around you. It energizes them, and encourages them to be clearer about their own feelings. Brain research shows that mothers and children bond through a primal mechanism known as *limbic resonance* that entrains two brains: the same emotional centers of the brain, the limbic region, are in sync, which leads to sharing biological rhythms, like heart rate and respiration. If they are truly entrained, mother and child can sense what each other is feeling, and even thinking, without an exchange of words. The same mechanism remains intact as we mature; you can entrain with others at a deep biological level, which includes sharing the openness of emotional freedom. Otherwise, stress and hidden negativity can serve to pull two people apart.

Shared Enthusiasm: Turn "this is great for me" into "this is great for all of us." Unless your enthusiasm reaches out to touch others, it may even have a negative effect. People aren't moved to help a leader if they don't think they are also helping themselves. (You can't help but wince and laugh at the smarmy manager in the television series *The Office* when he says, "The bad news is that there are going to be layoffs. The good news is that I'm being promoted.") Be sincere. Let your success be "our" success if it's deserved. Otherwise, the best maxim is not to look great but to let others make you great.

Genuine Caring for Others: Offering someone five minutes of praise and nodding "How's it going?" when you pass in the hall isn't the same as bonding. You have to care. The same conditions that you care about in your life apply to others. Look the person in the eye, forget everything else, and respond naturally.

Willingness to Build a Relationship: At bottom, all relationships are built on what two people have in common. The strongest adult bonds are between equals. You can't be part of everyone's family, but you can make others feel tied to you as a kindred spirit. At the soul level this is the only truth, because all souls are equal. It's the roles we play that enforce the illusion of inequality. As a leader, it's your job to play a role, but you must be attentive to stepping out of your role once in a while. Make contact for the sheer pleasure of it, for the fun of spending time together.

Reinforcing the Strengths of Others: Again and again it has been shown that the best leaders focus on the strengths of their followers. They build a team by assessing who does what well. They encourage each person to develop his or her best qualities. But that's just the beginning. People want to be praised for their strengths, specifically and personally. Walking past a machine operator and saying "Good job" is formulaic. Far better to know what he does well, point it out, and show that the job was worth doing.

Increasing the Self-esteem of Others: Self-esteem consists of three basic elements. People feel good about themselves, first, if they feel that they are doing good work at a job that is worthwhile; second, if they developed a positive self-image while growing up; and third, if they are living up to their core values. Knowing this, do your best to help those around you feel they are appreciated, and that they have every reason to appreciate themselves.

Nonviolent Communication: Removing any sense of threat allows you to manage situations in a way that fulfills people's needs. If you see stress, distrust, apathy, hidden hostility, or any other sign of resistance in the people you are communicating with, something is working against you on the emotional level. All change threatens the status quo. Inertia fights against vision. You can reduce the level of threat by looking at yourself closely and making sure that the following things are true:

> *You respect differences of opinion, even those that seem to undermine the success of your vision.*
> *You don't need others to change in order to be happy.*
> *You are coming from a place of peace.*
> *You genuinely want to understand why others are resisting you, without passing blame or judgment on them.*
> *You want change to benefit everyone, or as many people as possible.*

*You can walk away from setbacks without being
    hostile to those who oppose you today—they may
    become your allies tomorrow.*

Conflict Resolution: We are all emotionally involved in
our deepest beliefs. When two people cannot agree, the cause
is almost always at the feeling level: someone is stuck. Negotiation is the only way to move them. When you can negotiate with your opponents at the emotional level, the passion
behind your vision has a chance to speak to their hearts.

Using emotional intelligence as a negotiating tool requires the following:

*You respect the opposition, and you see that they feel
    respected.*

You remain firm but flexible.

*You genuinely feel that the other side has a right to
    their position.*

*Win-win is your ultimate goal. Everyone should walk
    away feeling they gained something.*

*You want the best for your opponents. Don't aim to
    get the most from them in terms of concessions.*

*You remove right and wrong from your vocabulary
    during the negotiations. Like it or not, everyone
    around the table feels equally righteous.*

*You see the other side of the coin, that every party feels
    equally aggrieved. A feeling of injustice doesn't
    exist on your side alone.*

*You speak personally, from the heart. This requires you
    to present yourself in a simple, appropriate, and
    balanced way.*

Agree to forgive and to ask for forgiveness. Let the
faults of others fade into the past while taking the
blame for your own faults here and now.

Never turn the argument to ideology or religion. These
are off limits, because no matter how diplomatic
you may be, the other party will feel threatened.

THE SEVEN SITUATIONS

Feelings either fulfill a need or they don't. A leader always keeps that in mind. She isn't here to encourage any emotion for its own sake. Each of the seven situations presented in the first chapter has an emotional side that is the best clue to the underlying need that must be filled. But you have to recognize it first.

1. Unfilled Need: To be safe and secure

Emotions: Fear, anxiety, uncertainty, feeling threatened
Your strategy: Bring the group's hidden anxiety out in the open. Provide your people with reasons not to be afraid. Lay out a path that will lead to stability. Ask those who are strongest to share the source of their strength. Promise that everyone will get through the crisis, and keep that promise as quickly as you can. Offer reassurance and help through one-on-one connections.

2. Unfilled Need: To Achieve, to Succeed

Emotions: Lack of motivation, apathy, sense of failure and inadequacy

Your strategy: Share your personal enthusiasm with the group. Reinforce their small successes. Make it clear that all victories are "our" victories. Describe the new possibilities that are opening up. Specify how each person can succeed according to his or her strengths. Assign a single task or project that is likely to succeed, making sure it's a success the person can be proud of.

3. Unfilled Need: To Cooperate with Others

Emotions: Jealousy, resentment, divisiveness, selfishness

Your strategy: Locate one emotion that everyone can share (pride, self-worth, satisfaction in doing one's best, mastery of a difficult task) and then ask for agreement on that feeling from everyone. Don't give up until agreement is reached. Bring up the topic of divisiveness without assigning blame. Point out the reasons why everybody wins if the group acts together. Be patient, but if you have to, weed out chronic complainers and backsliders. Negotiate differences by bringing rivals together in private. Give strong negative feedback to any public display of fractiousness.

4. Unfilled Need: To Nurture and Be Nurtured, to Belong

Emotions: Loneliness, isolation, feeling misunderstood and unheard

Your strategy: Show that you care about everyone in the group. The whole group is hurt when someone feels left out, but this feeling isn't something to discuss publicly. Sit down in private with the alienated member and hear what she has to say. Keep this contact going until she rejoins the group. Respect everyone's right to privacy, but make it clear that participation is mandatory. Show patience. Naturally, not everyone will participate to the same degree. Monitor the wallflowers by asking if they agree, and how they feel. Engage them, but don't confront them directly (e.g., "Adam, want to join the rest of us?" "It would be great if you had an idea, Alicia."). Instead, keep it simple and open-ended ("Adam, how does all of this sit with you?" "I'd like to hear what's on everyone's mind—Alicia?").

5. Unfilled Need: To Be Creative, to Grow

Emotions: Stagnatation, boredom, stifledness, feeling in a rut

Your strategy: Openly acknowledge to the group that a fresh wind must blow. Set time aside for blue-sky sessions, where everyone can let imagination run free. Make it clear that good new ideas will be rewarded. Never put down any sign of creativity and imagination. Don't point out obstacles, budgetary limits, or impracticalities. Do surprising things that bring smiles. Say "astonish me" and mean it—you want everyone to stretch and feel safe when they do.

6. Unfilled Need: To Be Guided by Core Values

Emotions: Guilt, emptiness, lack of guidance, aimlessness

Your strategy: Speak to the group from the heart. Inspire from the soul. Share personal stories about peak experiences in your life. Ask for the same from others. Don't step on other people's moral values or act self-righteous about yours. Focus on the unlimited potential for growth in everyone. Put your highest values—compassion, love, loyalty, honesty, and integrity—into practice by acting as role model. If it seems appropriate, ask for group silence, meditation, or prayer. Don't be afraid of an uplifting moment. Always be straightforward. Appreciate the innocence hidden in everyone.

7. Need: To Be Spiritually Fulfilled

Emotions: Yearning, seeking, the desire for more from life

Your strategy: The word *strategy* isn't really appropriate in this case. You are here to spread the light, and you do that by being in the light. You understand and accept all people. You feel compassion in all situations. Now you can spread your influence simply by being. If you have found your soul, your source in pure consciousness, people will sense your state of bliss and unity, lifting their spirits without effort on your part. Through you, they will sense that inner peace and complete safety are possible.

A ROSE CAN CHANGE A LIFE

Let me tell you a story about how I saw for myself the power of emotional bonds. When I was a boy growing up in India, my father was an army doctor stationed in Jabalpur, a large town close to the center of the country. On one particular day the whole of Jabalpur was aroused to a fever pitch by news of an impending visit by India's prime minister, Jawaharlal Nehru. India had been born as a country in 1947, just a few months after I was born, and as its first elected leader, Nehru was somewhere between a father and a saint to the Indian people.

As Nehru's motorcade approached on the appointed day, a ripple of awe and excitement ran through the streets as if Gandhi himself were coming, and indeed Nehru had inherited Gandhi's mantle. I remember our neighbors climbing lampposts just to catch a glimpse of Nehru's car; treetops along the street sagged under the weight of little boys hanging from their branches. My mother had dressed in her best sari, and it didn't matter whom she had turned to—a maid, a best friend, or the wife of the head of hospital where my father worked—nobody could talk about anything but Nehru.

When the motorcade finally wound its way through the streets, it passed directly in front of our house. Then something remarkable happened. My mother had found a place in the front of the crowd. Earlier she had confided to us that she was certain Nehru would notice her among the tens of thousands thronging his route, and although we had teased her, her confidence remained unshaken. And when the moment came, she actually *did* catch Nehru's eye! He paused for a second, and then reached for the single red rose he always wore in his lapel. He tossed it to her. Even in all the tumult my mother caught it, and when the parade was over, she took it inside and carefully placed it in her best vase.

All that afternoon our house was filled with people coming over to marvel at the rose, the kind you could buy in the market stalls for a few rupees. But because Nehru had thrown it with his own hands, it had taken on his mystical status. And because my mother had caught it, so had she. People who saw her every day now lowered their voices to a whisper in her presence and looked on her with reverence. And when I looked at my mother, I saw that her brush with greatness seemed to have given her a new sense of herself, too. At the day's end Nehru's rose was saved for posterity, carefully pressed between the pages of a book like a sacred relic.

Imagine yourself inspiring that kind of love and loyalty. It's what every successful visionary does.

Political greatness comes to only a few, but most of us will find some leadership opportunities at our place of work, where it's not unusual to find a vacuum of emotional intelligence. In an extensive study of worker satisfaction, the Gallup research organization found that the workplace remains very impersonal. According to Gallup, just 17 percent of employees report that their manager "has made an investment in our relationship." You don't have to be the leader of a nation to heal this situation!

SPIRITUAL INTELLIGENCE

With the last two needs—for higher guidance and for spiritual fulfillment—we move beyond emotional intelligence. At this deeper level we are working in the realm of *spiritual intelligence,* which gets us in touch with love, compassion, joy, and inner peace. These values are transpersonal. They belong to humanity as a whole. Spiritual intelligence doesn't address one specific situation. It's about finding the sacred in everyday life. You come from a place of love, joy, and equanimity because you are in touch with your own soul.

Spiritual intelligence is a matter not of learning skills but of finding who you are at the soul level. We are all conscious; we all know what it's like to have inner peace, silence, trust, and joy. Where do these experiences come from? If they come from the very core of our being, from the soul, then it's only natural to want to go there and experience ourselves.

Exploring who you are at a deeper level than your everyday thoughts is the true definition of meditation. At the beginning it's enough to practice a simple meditation like the one that follows:

Meditation on the Breath

Set aside twenty minutes in the morning and the evening when you can sit alone in a quiet place without being interrupted or disturbed. Turn off your phone and your beeper. Close your eyes and do nothing for five minutes, letting your breathing rate settle naturally. Observe your mind chattering away, but don't interact with it. Let your thoughts and feelings simply be what they are.

Now place your attention gently in the middle of your chest. As you do, follow your breath as it goes in and out. Feel each exhalation as if it were releasing the breath from your whole body; feel each inhalation as if it were spreading your in-breath to every part of your body. Don't impose a tempo on your breathing, fast or slow. Don't try for deep or shallow breaths, but have the intention that over time your breathing will become subtler and more refined. Continue this meditation for fifteen minutes. It's okay to fall asleep: this just means you have to catch up on your rest before you can meditate. At the end of the session, take a minute to come out of the meditative state; don't jump immediately into action.

Getting comfortable with this simple practice is taking the first big step toward spiritual intelligence. By meditating every day, you will allow the soul to infuse daily life. As this happens, you will see a host of changes in yourself, such as:

> *Unexpected moments of joy*
> *A sense of peace in the midst of activity*

The ability to see yourself clearly
More reasons to appreciate others, and fewer reasons to
   criticize
Less need to control
Greater trust that the right answers will appear
A willingness to go with the flow
A deep sense of belonging

Once you begin to have such experiences, you will effortlessly and naturally extend them outside yourself. It will become clear to you that whatever is inside you must be inside everyone. At the level of the soul, everyone possesses the same qualities. The spiritually intelligent leader acts on these qualities even when they may not be much in evidence. She gives each person space to change. One might call this attitude "nurturing in silence." At this point a leader has gone beyond the immediate situation; she is accepting fully the one role that matters most, to be the soul of the group.

When emotional intelligence merges with spiritual intelligence, human nature is transformed. Such a leader embodies what every wisdom tradition calls "the light." The light gives rise to love and compassion, even when the person shows no outward signs of acting from the soul. Rather, the invisible powers of Being—the pure consciousness at the base of all existence—begin to show that they are real. Struggle gives way to ease, and conflict yields to complete trust that the best outcome will manifest. Your slightest desire is supported by the universe and made manifest. Every action is part of the flow of life. The first day you meditate, you open a doorway to the light. You ask your soul for more awareness, and your wish is granted. The soul is nothing but light, yet that is a metaphor—the real substance of the soul is awareness.

Awareness is unlimited. The emotional bonds that link you to another person are bonds of light. At the soul level you are already united. Your role as a leader is to help others see that this is so.

THE LESSONS OF EMOTIONAL BONDING

- Leading from the soul means bonding with others so that they want to share in your vision and be fulfilled through your shared success.
- Once you value emotional intelligence, you can learn the skills that bond people together. This requires you to build relationships and give of yourself.
- As a leader from the soul, you perceive the emotions hidden in any situation and show how to repair them. You know with certainty that everyone is already bonded at the soul level.

WHAT TO DO TODAY

Emotional intelligence grows through perception. Look around at your present situation (at work, in the family, with close friends) and observe it from the level of feeling. Your heart will tell you when other people are emotionally distant from you. The signs are hidden or obvious tension; the other people don't seem relaxed; they don't laugh with you, or look you in the eye. They don't seem to want to be around you or share in your success. How can you turn this distance into a bond?

Today your assignment is to take on the task of changing the emotional tone in your life wherever it isn't working. Look at the behaviors listed below. Pick one to apply today, and over the course of the next month choose each of the ten behaviors at least once.

Closing the Gap

TEN BEHAVIORS FOR MENDING EMOTIONAL DISTANCE

1. Notice where another person is strong or talented, and point it out to him.
2. Compliment him on getting better at something.
3. Praise him without expecting praise in return.
4. Go along with his wishes when it feels right in your heart.
5. If the heat gets to be too much, walk away, but then come back in a conciliatory mood.
6. Own your own feelings. Nobody else does. And accept that you don't own the other person's feelings: he does.
7. Don't bring up sensitive issues when they could be embarrassing (especially in front of other people or the whole group).
8. Before bringing up a personal issue, wait until you're in a good emotional place, and then make sure the other person is in a good place, too.

9. Avoid stale rituals. If you find yourself saying the same rote things day after day, that's a ritual, not a genuine response. Find something new to say, and some new way to show you care.

10. Find one thing every day to forgive the other person for. Don't let him know what it is; just forgive him, and let it go.

As you apply these behaviors on a daily basis, turning emotional distance into a bond, be easy with yourself and with the other person. Be sincere; don't overdo it. Above all, don't do it because you want to be right or to prove that you can make someone like you; your aim is more objective than that. You aim to develop the emotional intelligence necessary to go beyond your old unhealthy patterns. To value emotional bonding is to bring yourself and someone you care about in from the cold, even if it doesn't directly benefit you.

Emotionally speaking, you have only three kinds of situations with people: those you can fix, those you put up with, and those you must walk away from. As a leader, it's your duty to find as many ways to fix a situation as you can. Most people put up with too much, and when they reach a point of unbearable frustration, they walk out. By contrast, you can fix a situation through emotional intelligence and skillful coping with emotions. By closing the gap that isolates people from one another, you are proving that the emotional side of life can be fruitful. Overcoming our fear and inner resistance leads to shared joy.

Three

A = AWARENESS

Awareness is the birthplace of possibility. Everything you want to do, everything you want to be, starts here. To be a successful visionary, you must be as aware as possible. At every moment, many paths lead forward. Awareness tells you which is the right one to take.

As a leader, your own awareness affects everyone around you. Those whom you lead and serve depend on your grasp of the situation. You must reach inside for the right response. You alone can raise the group's awareness from lower needs to higher needs. To do that, you first must fulfill each need in yourself.

Awareness is a synonym for consciousness. There is no limit to what you can change, because consciousness brings light to every aspect of life. But if your consciousness is constricted, everything else will be, too. On the other hand, if you are in a state of expanded awareness, everything else will expand. The most ancient wisdom traditions say, "Know that one thing by which all else is known." That one thing is consciousness itself. Nothing has a greater power of transformation.

Awareness is the birthplace of possibility. Everything you want to achieve begins here. As a new idea arises, it must gather power and influence. Other people must want to support it: the means to turn vision into reality must come to hand. All of these things depend on your awareness, because the moment you have a new idea, many paths lead to the future. At a deep place inside you, the right path calls out. The successful visionary looks inside, day after day, to find the next step in that path. For her, success is an evolving journey.

Awareness isn't the same as thinking. The world is so complex that the rational mind cannot calculate all the possibilities in a given situation. Instinctively, we all know this. Therefore we don't really use logic and reason the way we say we do. We make our decisions intuitively, and afterward we bring in logic and reason to justify our choices. This doesn't mean that logic isn't valuable. It means that we use much more of our awareness than we realize.

Brain research shows that even in the simplest decisions, many centers of the brain are involved, particularly the emotional centers. When you look at a banana in the grocery store, a cashmere scarf in a department store, or a used car at a dealership, you may be silently calculating what you think is a fair price. Within seconds you will have made a judgment, yet you are barely aware, if at all, of what your brain has done. One shopper will think it's fair to pay two dollars a pound for organic bananas while another will pass them by at that price. If asked why, each could probably give you a reason, but at the moment of decision, multiple influences were at work. It would take a long time to verbalize these processes, even without accounting for how they intermingle and weigh against one another.

As a leader, you must make decisions the way a shopper chooses bananas, using many centers of your brain. Most leadership training programs hold the opposite to be true. Reason and logic are purported to dominate; 90 percent of decision making is supposedly based on analysis. But behavioral research indicates that when we make decisions, much more is going on in the brain.

In one experiment, subjects were shown photos with strong emotional content, both positive and negative (a newborn baby, a wedding, a train wreck, a battle scene). Their brains were being scanned, and the photos lit up the emotional center of the brain, the amygdala. Then the subjects were asked how much they would be willing to pay for simple household items. Consistently, these subjects were willing to pay much more than subjects who hadn't been emotionally stimulated beforehand. And this held true whether the photos had aroused positive or negative emotions. Feeling happier made them willing to pay up to three and four times what they would normally pay, but so would feeling depressed. Even more telling, the experimenters could not eliminate the emotional influence on decisions, no matter how hard they tried. The ideal of the completely rational solution is an illusion.

This is probably a very good thing, for if you could rely solely on reason and logic, you would be depriving yourself of the unseen power of your awareness. Awareness is a synonym for consciousness. In the world's great spiritual traditions, consciousness is considered an attribute of God and is therefore infinite and omnipresent. The divine sees and knows everything. That is why the Vedic sages of India instruct us to "know that one thing by which all else is known." They are referring to consciousness. Yet even in secular terms, through brain studies like the one described above, we know that consciousness is vast and largely untapped. The thinking mind is only the tip of the iceberg.

THE SEVEN ATTRIBUTES OF CONSCIOUSNESS

Although you can only think about one thing at a time, your awareness is silently functioning on many levels. A leader takes full advantage of this fact by speaking to those hidden levels. Consciousness delivers the following personal attributes, in ascending order:

> *Centeredness*
> *Self-motivation*
> *Coherence*
> *Intuition, insight*
> *Creativity*
> *Inspiration*
> *Transcendence*

You may recognize that these attributes match the seven needs that a leader must fulfill. The best leaders are always a step ahead of the group in the hierarchy of needs. When the group is beginning to feel safe and secure, the leader is already thinking about achievement. When the group is starting to enjoy success, the leader is already thinking about team building, and so on up the ladder. The greatest leaders are tuned in to all seven levels, which prepares them for any situation in advance. If you aspire to lead from the soul, you must have personal experience of these seven attributes of consciousness.

Centeredness: Awareness is stable and secure within itself, needing no support from the outside. When you are in contact with this quality, you are unshakable in a crisis. While others around you feel insecure and unsafe, you are centered. In this hour of need, you are prepared to relieve the anxiety of those around you and bring out their best qualities.

Self-motivation: Awareness is imbued with the quality of self-referral, which means that it finds everything it needs within itself. From this inner source of awareness, confidence and energy come naturally, and the supply of both is endless. When you are in contact with this quality of awareness, you have no doubt that success is possible. While others see danger, you see hidden opportunities. This ability to unfold a path to success prepares you to lead when achievement is the main goal.

Coherence: Awareness is orderly and self-organizing. It receives streams of raw input from the five senses and forms them into a coherent picture of the world. When you are in contact with this quality, you can inspire others to come together around your vision—whether it's building a new teen center in town, reorganizing the local PTA thrift shop, or training animals to visit sick children in hospital to give them a lift. In place of confusion and conflict, you see a clear, united purpose. This ability makes you a leader capable of bringing people together in support of your idea.

Intuition, insight: Awareness is always observing. It's observing you reading these words right now. But unlike your everyday torrent of thoughts, this awareness is unclouded by personal bias; it sees reality instead of illusion. When you are aware, you understand the situation directly, without having to think too much. Insight comes spontaneously. You are adept at dealing with people because you understand what they need—perhaps more clearly than they do themselves. This makes you a leader when the goal is to make each person feel understood and listened to.

Creativity: Awareness is the meeting point between the unknown and the known. It converts dim possibilities into new realities. When you are aware, you feel comfortable with uncertainty—you thrive on it, in fact, because you realize that unpredictability is part of the very fabric of being. It is the essence of innovation, and you love to explore and discover new ways of doing things. When you are aware, you can lead others by encouraging them to see beyond the old ways of doing things, and you can offer them the sheer excitement of replacing their outworn perspectives.

Inspiration: Awareness is rooted in love, compassion, faith, and virtue. According to some of the great wisdom traditions, everything that exists arises from an endless sea of awareness, or consciousness. That is also true of these fundamental human qualities. We may lose sight of them, but they are no less there. No one had to invent love and compassion: they arise from that sea of conscious awareness. When you are aware, you can inspire others. You help them see their better selves, and by doing so, you lift them up. At a time when people hunger for personal transformation and redemption, you are well placed to make a difference.

Transcendence: Awareness ultimately has no boundaries. It exists in this world but endlessly goes beyond it. The world's great wisdom traditions all derive from a higher reality that is indescribable but can be experienced. This is the greatest wonder and source of awe. As the ancient India sages declare, "This isn't knowledge that you learn. It's knowledge that you become." When you fully absorb this insight, you know what it means to transcend. You don't need to travel anywhere; all of reality exists in you. You exemplify wholeness because you are united with everything and everyone around you. You exist to demonstrate that human beings can reach the infinite, and by simply being who you are, you help others get there.

RAISING THE GROUP

As a leader, you try to raise group consciousness from its present level to the next highest one in the hierarchy. This process is cumulative—it works only if it can build on the previous step—so make sure to start at the beginning. Don't take anything for granted. Step by step, you can unfold the seven attributes of consciousness, as follows:

Centeredness: This silent aspect of consciousness gives us a strong sense of self. When a group is at this level, everyone feels secure.

Exercise: One of the simplest techniques for becoming centered uses body awareness. Ask the group to sit still and take a moment to get in touch with their bodies, to relax into the simple state of being physically present. Ask the group to become aware of areas of comfort and discomfort.

As a variation on this basic technique, ask the group to sit quietly and become aware of their breathing. Ask people to pay attention, gently and easily, to their breath as it flows in and out. Another alternative is to become aware of the heart. Ask them to sit quietly and to bring their focus, easily and gently, on the area of the chest beneath the breastbone. The aim here isn't to listen to their heartbeat, but to be in contact with the heart as a center of emotion. Let whatever feelings or sensations that arise be what they are. If you feel self-conscious about leading a group in this way, you can show people these exercises in one-on-one sessions. There are very few groups that wouldn't benefit from these techniques for becoming more centered, which also have the beneficial effect of reducing stress.

Self-motivation: This aspect of consciousness inspires achievement. When a group rises to this level, everyone feels that they have an equal opportunity to succeed.

Exercise: Announce that the best motivation is to work from each person's strengths, and to do that, we need to know what those strengths are. Divide the group into pairs, handing out pencil and paper. Have each partner write down three strengths she sees in the other person. To get things rolling, offer some possibilities: "My partner is good at coming up with ideas, making others feel comfortable, scheduling and organization, being productive, meeting deadlines, negotiation, persuasion, innovation, etc." If people are new to the group, have them write down their own strengths.

After five minutes have the pairs exchange lists. The two partners will now discuss the strengths that were noted. Modify these if there are doubts or disagreements. Then have the pairs draw up action plans that would maximize those strengths. (A simple format would be: "To better use my strength, which is _____, I suggest the following: _____.") The goal here is to match each person with what she is best at, and then to show that you intend to utilize her strengths. This is an effective way to spark motivation. When someone feels that her strengths have been recognized and will be put to use, her motivation to perform will naturally increase.

Coherence: This aspect of consciousness bridges differences. Group coherence means that everyone is pulling together and shares the same goals.

Exercise: Realistically, it's not easy to get a fractured, divided group to pull together into a cohesive team. But you don't have to accomplish this right away. Instead, ask the team to divide into pairs of their own choosing. Each pair will work as a partnership. They don't have to share the same tasks, but they will share everything else, from positive things (like the progress being made) to negative things (like frustration and obstacles to progress). Each person will thus be a sounding board and a source of feedback.

The point isn't to assign one person's work to two but to create a bond between partners who care, help, and share. At their first meeting, each pair should agree on what benefit they want to get from being partners. They should meet once a day for a few minutes if possible, or at least three times a week. At the end of the week the whole group gets together for an informal verbal report on how each pair is doing. Then the group can move on to a general discussion of how their overall goal is coming along. By using pairs instead of trying to bring coherence to a large group, you are creating bonds at the most personal level.

Intuition, insight: This aspect of consciousness generates empathy. When a group rises to this level, each person feels understood.

Exercise: Divide the group into pairs again, putting

together people who are not close friends. (There's a reason for this.) In fact, strangers would be the best choice, if possible. Sitting quietly in relative privacy, each person tells the other something he has never told anyone before. It shouldn't be a deep, dark secret or a source of guilt and shame—more like something that has been on his mind that he hasn't had a chance to say. The next step is to discuss each other's disclosure. One person may ask the other for advice with whatever issue he's raised, but that's not necessary. The point of the exercise is to be heard and understood.

As the leader, you may feel that sharing confidences is too personal. In that case, have each pair fill in the blank in the following sentence: "The thing I want others to understand about me is _____." All but the most reserved person will be happy to answer this question. To follow up, meet again as pairs a week later and discuss whether each person feels more understood.

Creativity: This aspect of consciousness unfolds the future in new ways. When a group rises to this level, it embraces the new.

Exercise: Creativity is an aspect of personal freedom, so find out if the people in your group feel free to let their creative juices flow. Hand out the following self-assessment, asking each person to fill it out anonymously.

CREATIVITY QUESTIONNAIRE

Part 1: In the interests of making our team more creative, please answer the following questions by circling Yes, No, or Neutral.

Yes No Neutral   The rules are loose enough for me to breathe.

Yes No Neutral   I'm appreciated.

Yes No Neutral   There is minimal pressure to conform.

Yes No Neutral   Things are not too organized.

Yes No Neutral   People are having fun around here.

Yes No Neutral   New ideas excite those in charge.

Yes No Neutral   New ideas move up the ladder quickly.

Yes No Neutral   Risk is equated with reward.

Yes No Neutral   I'm allowed to be independent in choosing assignments.

Yes No Neutral   There's room for play.

Yes No Neutral   I am given time to myself.

Yes No Neutral   I admire what the group stands for.

Part 2: Choosing from the above list, rank in order the three things that would enable you to be more creative.

#1 _____

#2 _____

#3 _____

Collect the questionnaires and tote up the number of Yes, No, and Neutral responses for each item. At the same time, list the three choices in Part 2 that got the most votes. The next time the group meets, hand out the results for discussion. You will have a good snapshot of how creative everyone feels. You should also have a good idea of where the quickest improvements can be made.

Inspiration: This aspect of consciousness brings about inner change. When a group rises to this level, all the members feel that they have found their true calling.

Exercise: The longest-lasting inspiration comes from within. Ask each person to come up with a role model or archetype whom he or she finds truly inspiring, and to write down the person's name. The aim is to help people express the same qualities of that archetype. For example, one quality may be the love embodied in Jesus, the compassion of Buddha, the peaceful strength of Gandhi, the wisdom of Athena, the power of Wonder Woman. Have them write down the specific qualities that are most precious to them in their archetypes. Ask them to become the incarnation of these qualities.

Here's my own personal program for inspiration. I have set aside a special place in my home for meditation, and there I surround myself with images of my archetype. (Actually, I have several archetypes, one of which is Krishna, the Hindu deity.) When I finish my daily meditation, I open my eyes and look at these images, focusing on Krishna's strength, love, and all-encompassing wisdom. Quietly I ask for these qualities to increase in me. Knowing that all archetypes are symbols of consciousness, I am using Krishna to stand in for aspects of my own awareness. It is these aspects that I want to increase.

As you can see, this exercise isn't directly related to a project or group goal. But if your group has risen to the level where everyone is comfortable revealing their need for higher guidance, they can share their own inspiring stories of personal growth and cherished role models. At this point every aspect of consciousness is being enhanced because the closer you get to the soul level, the more the invisible power of awareness can benefit you.

Transcendence: This aspect of consciousness brings liberation. When a group rises to this level, enlightenment is their shared goal.

Exercise: Traditionally, people reach enlightenment through spiritual discipline, most especially through long, deep meditation. Nothing could be more individual. But three aspects of the spiritual path can be shared very productively:

> *Be of service together.*
> *Share wisdom together.*
> *Become a community in spirit.*

Every wisdom tradition has espoused these three practices, which reflect the same thing, really: the knowledge that each of us is more than our limited mind and body; we are part of the infinite consciousness that generates and governs the universe. Therefore each practice is a way of going beyond the small, limited self.

When you are of service, you value others as you value yourself, making their needs your own. When you share wisdom—through reading and contemplating the world's scriptures—you show that your real allegiance is to the soul. When you organize as a community in spirit, you declare that living from the level of the soul can peacefully unite people from any background. The overall effect is to rise to a higher level of existence, the level embodied by the greatest saints and sages. They represent the ultimate in successful visionaries.

AWARENESS CAN TRANSFORM

Nothing has more power to transform than awareness. When you become complete inside yourself, the worst conditions in the world don't matter. A few years ago I took a boat to Robben Island, which lies off Cape Town, South Africa. Continuously pounded by an Atlantic surf heavy enough to break apart any ship unlucky enough to run aground on it, this island was once considered the perfect place to isolate lepers. A prison was built there for political prisoners, one of whom would be Nelson Mandela.

In 1964 Mandela was convicted of sabotage and of taking part in various antiapartheid activities. Fortunate to escape hanging, he received a sentence of life imprisonment instead. Today visitors can see for themselves the tiny jail cell with its iron cot where Nelson Mandela spent eighteen years of his life. The only other furniture is a small table and a covered can that served as a toilet.

Walking around the prison grounds, which are now preserved as a memorial to the freedom movement, one still feels the heavy air of oppression. Daily life for Mandela was the lowest of the low. Because his offense was political, and because he was black, Mandela was given the worst and most meager rations. For the first fifteen years of his imprisonment, before he was given a bed, he slept on the floor. He performed hard labor in a limestone quarry, and he was allowed one letter and one visitor every six months.

How did such a great leader emerge from such inhuman conditions? To speak of ordinary motivation would be to miss the point. Motivation temporarily raises your spirits, but it is difficult to sustain. Inspiration is more durable, and Mandela's inspiration came from his remarkable awareness, which he chose to develop further during his ordeal. Mandela went into prison as a hot-headed rebel who condoned violence. He emerged after twenty-seven years a transformed man, still firm in his intentions, but having renounced violence and having transcended the pitfalls of hatred and bitterness. Guided by his enlightened consciousness, the African National Conference shifted its emphasis away from black domination and toward the creation of a united country that included all races, with malice toward none.

As the father of a free South Africa, which was born without the bloodbath that had always been predicted, Mandela rose to the stature of a secular saint. But the personal qualities he developed sprang from a source we all have in common: awareness. This is the source of insight, nurturing, inspiration, and transcendence—all qualities that emerge when a leader's awareness expands. They are available to you, too. The seeds of greatness were planted in you the very moment you were granted consciousness. If you follow the inward path using truth and clarity as your compass points, the outer world cannot help but respond to your intention. Its exact responses may be unpredictable, but through its support the rightness of the path will be proved to you again and again.

The Lessons of Awareness

- Leading from the soul means expanding your awareness in order to meet the needs of others. As you become more aware, invisible powers begin to support your vision.
- Consciousness has its own innate qualities. Once you cultivate them in yourself, you can raise the consciousness of those you lead and serve.
- The ultimate goal of awareness is to be transformed. Beyond any specific desire is the overarching need to become completely liberated. When you reach that point, you and your vision are one.

WHAT TO DO TODAY

Awareness is innate—you don't have to seek it outside yourself. But expanded awareness must be cultivated.

Today you can start out on the path to unlimited awareness. The steps are simple, as you'll see below. You don't have to adopt the whole program all at once. Return to this section as a road map. Wherever you are starting from, the path to higher consciousness is always open.

Your Awareness Program

Stop struggling.
Keep listening to your inner voice.
Meditate in order to reach the core of your awareness.
Test your boundaries.
Remain centered.
Look beyond your personal beliefs.
Gather information from every source.
Learn to have clear intentions.
Value inner peace.

Even though awareness is invisible, taking these steps will make the benefits of expanded awareness evident very quickly. Let's take a close look at each of these ways to expand your awareness.

Stop struggling: The first step is to realize that life isn't meant to be a struggle, and what makes a leader isn't toughness in the face of obstacles. Rather, you could help others see that it is possible to find support within themselves, taking advantage of the smoothest, shortest, and least effortful way to reach results. Until you actually test a new way of doing things—the way of expanded awareness—you will only be putting window dressing on your old belief system.

Keep listening to your inner voice: No matter how skilled you become at dealing with challenges, in the end every decision gets tested inside. Whether you call it listening to your gut or obeying that little voice inside you, the process is the same. But not every inner voice is the same, or equally reliable. A leader pierces through layers of second-hand opinion, stress, anxiety, groupthink, and the welter of opinions both within and without. Only when she finds the voice inside herself that is almost silent has she located the voice that should be listened to. Start finding that voice today.

Meditate to reach the core of your awareness: The practice of meditation has enormous implications for awareness. Waiting inside you is a level of silent being. It is the source of your awareness and the womb of creation. All solutions exist here, as well as all possibilities. When you meditate and reach this level of yourself, something magical happens. All boundaries disappear. If you could maintain this boundless state permanently, you would achieve enlightenment, which is nothing more than residing in the state of pure awareness, where all possibilities coexist in this moment and in every moment. Although very few of us ever attain enlightenment, you and I can still experience that boundless state for a brief time. Every visit to this level of your consciousness refreshes your mind and body like nothing else.

Test your boundaries: Becoming more aware is an internal process, but that doesn't mean it's passive. Meditation and turning within can also serve as very powerful agents of change in the outside world. They can significantly improve your life, as well as help you fulfill the needs of others. When you step out of your meditation and back into the arena of stress, turbulence, emotional conflict, confusion, and competition, do so with this intention: *I want to see what I am made of.* What you are made of isn't a given. It changes every day. And yet the underlying aspect of awareness remains ever the same.

I am not suggesting that you plunge into ordeals that will overwhelm your awareness. Testing means checking a boundary to see if it has moved. Even a slight shift is enough. You don't have to overcome massive resistance or prove yourself. Quite the opposite, in fact—what you're doing here is expanding your comfort zone. As awareness expands, so do the areas in which you feel strong, confident, and capable.

Remain centered: Your center is your place of power. When you remain there, the universe will channel everything you need. It's as if your actions were superfluid, a term used in physics to describe the state of no resistance and no friction. Leaders who handle crises exceptionally well aren't keeping their heads so much as they are keeping centered. How is that done? First you need to know what it feels like to be centered, if you don't already. As discussed, meditation is a good way to experience this state. Being centered comes naturally to all of us, and you can recognize it by the following indications:

> *Your mind is quiet. Mental chatter is gone.*
> *You feel safe and confident.*
> *Your mood is carefree.*
> *You have a strong sense of being.*
> *You feel a quiet but intense energy from being alive.*
> *Your attention is fully in the present moment.*

Everyone has experienced such a state from time to time. It's up to you to cultivate it. Then when you find yourself in difficult situations, when there are forces pulling you in all directions, you can locate the quiet zone inside that you have grown familiar with. You will have access to your place of power, the still point in a turning world.

Look beyond your personal beliefs: The stronger your beliefs, the narrower your viewpoint. Strongly held beliefs are a sign of restrictive boundaries and constricted awareness. We all harbor a mental image of leaders being pillars of strength who cannot be shaken from their core beliefs, and in some situations, such as wars or major political upheavals, such leaders may be necessary. But in the end it's the person who is flexible, who can see the situation from all sides and is alert to subtle changes, who succeeds best. Being able to see beyond your personal beliefs is a vital step in actually going beyond those boundaries. Your attitude should be "I think I'm right, but that doesn't mean I see the whole picture."

Gather information from every source: There's a big difference between being centered and being self-centered. When you are centered, information flows in from all directions. You function as the switchboard, gathering as many viewpoints as you can. But when you are self-centered, ego takes over. You become convinced that your idea must be the best simply because it's yours. At first this is a difficult distinction to make. Most leaders are afraid to seem weak or uncertain. They place such a high value on being decisive that they find it hard to take in other opinions. But the more viewpoints you absorb, the wider your awareness will be.

A great leader practices what appears to be a peculiar kind of alchemy. He listens to everyone around him, taking in all each has to offer; but when it comes time to make a final decision, he stands behind it with total conviction. There is no magic involved, actually. If you are centered, you won't be shaken by contending opinions; you will become wiser for them. If you aren't centered, the opposite happens: the more voices you listen to, the more you vacillate. As a leader, you must learn that if you want to avoid indecision, the answer isn't to make up your mind alone and insist on your way or the highway. The answer is to become open to all influences, but be swayed by none.

Learn to have clear intentions: A good leader is comfortable giving orders and having them carried out. A great leader goes one step further: he has an intention, takes steps to realize it, and then lets go of the outcome. Action is still required. You don't just make a wish and blow out a candle. But because it resides at the deepest level of awareness, intention is a very powerful thing. Having expressed a completely clear intention from the deepest level of awareness, or consciousness, you expect the forces of nature to support you, and as they do, you obey the signals that the situation sends to you. Perhaps you will have to do very little, or you may have to fight against tremendous odds. Both extremes are possible. But what is really happening is that your intention is leading to a result.

Our society, which is materialistic, doesn't teach us that intentions have their own power, although we are told to "follow our dreams," which is roughly what a clear intention is—a core desire, or dream, that leads you on day by day. Beyond this vague notion of following a dream, you must realize that intentions come true when the following conditions are ripe:

> *You desire from a deep level of awareness.*
> *Your desire is true to who you are.*
> *You trust that the universe can bring about the result you want.*
> *You let go and don't force the issue.*
> *You resolve your inner conflict and confusion.*
> *You remain alert to receive any feedback, however faint.*
> *You tune in to find out what is needed next.*

Rarely when you put in a penny does the candy machine spit out the reward you seek (although sometimes things turn out this way). The path to making any desire come true is to be aware every step of the way. Begin to walk this path now. Small intentions lead the way, but even the greatest wishes are achieved through the same steps.

Value inner peace: In this society we proudly announce how much coffee we drink, and we celebrate our status as adrenaline junkies. Surrounded by chaos and stress, people often mistake being excited for truly feeling alive. There's no denying that a surge of adrenaline can give you a great high—for a few hours. As the adrenaline ebbs, however, body and mind are exhausted, and over time the negative effects of stress take their toll. It's a dead-end strategy to think that you must be as amped up as your surroundings. Nobody thrives on stress, no matter how convinced they are otherwise. The most productive state of being is peace. Many leaders find this hard to learn. They trade the present for the future, throwing themselves into chaotic situations with a promise that one day, years from now, they will have time to rest.

This is a devil's bargain. Peace is either here in this moment or it doesn't exist. By peace I don't mean passivity. Peace has nothing to do with lethargy or lack of involvement. True peace is a vibrant state. It's alive with potential and the expectation of great things to come. It's the moment just before birth brings new life. The first step to achieving such peace is to value it. Awareness brings you more of whatever you value—that's a basic rule of consciousness. So by valuing the state of peace with its inner silence, you invite it to become part of your daily life.

As your awareness expands, you will become of greater service to the world. Because we are so used to leaders being authority figures, it's hard to accept that to lead is to serve. But this becomes second nature once you realize that service isn't self-sacrifice—it's the effortless expression of your state of awareness. (I'm reminded of an aphorism, "I can't hear what you're saying because who you are is deafening.") So who are you? You are your awareness, in every fiber of your being.

Four

D = DOING

A leader is action-oriented. Only through action can you bring a vision to life. But vision and action must be compatible; to make them so requires skill. That skill begins with walking the walk, energizing others around you, and recruiting them to your mission.

Every situation calls out for the right action. As a leader, you must identify the role you are expected to play. If you are aware, your role will call out to you. Successful visionaries are able to fulfill any role—their flexibility comes from the soul's infinite flexibility.

Doing is different when you lead from the soul. It turns into nondoing, which is the same as allowing. You step aside and let your soul act through you, without struggle, worry, or resistance. Nondoing isn't the same as doing nothing. It's the most powerful way to lead, because you trust that your soul wants to bring the best possible outcome. Your role is to tune in and witness how perfectly life can organize itself when the soul is in charge.

We have been focusing on the vision aspect of "successful visionary," but there can be no success without action. Once a leader points the way, everyone is expected to follow her direction. The burden of leadership is that outcomes are always unpredictable. The most common complaint one hears from leaders is that every minute of the day they must choose between one course of action and another. This leaves them almost no time to cultivate the deepest level of the self. In a world where the future cannot be controlled, however, it's foolhardy to ignore the very source of action, which is the core of one's being, the soul.

By now you are far ahead of most leaders. You've learned the hidden power of emotional bonding, and you know the value of expanded awareness. Your actions, when grounded this deeply, will come directly from your vision. But you also face the challenge of making your actions as effective as possible. Doing is a skill. It is based on five steps that make the difference between success and failure. Whenever you are in a position to lead:

1. Be action-oriented. The atmosphere around you must be dynamic. Everyone in the group should feel energized by the call to action.

2. Act as a role model. Be willing to do the same things you ask others to do. That way you will recruit others to act. A leader doesn't have to perform the jobs he assigns; if you can, however, that's a great advantage. A leader serves as a role model in giving of himself completely.

3. Commit yourself to good, honest feedback. Show that you want to hear the truth, and when you give feedback to others, be candid but positive. Emphasize their contributions first and foremost.

4. Be persistent. There will always be setbacks and obstacles. The course of any significant project never ran smoothly. When others are secretly worrying about failure, your unflagging persistence is a strong asset.

5. Take time to celebrate. Every time there's a significant achievement, create an atmosphere of celebration around it. Work and nothing but work will eventually deplete people's enthusiasm. By celebrating signposts along the way to final success, you give everyone a taste of that success in advance.

A visionary leader won't be satisfied with building a team of competent, skilled people. Important as that surely is, it's even more vital to show the group—and the world at large—that your actions are authentic. Every time you stand up in a group, you affirm the truth voiced by Italo Magni, prize-winning public speaker: "If you're talking with your head, you're going to speak to their heads. If you're talking with your heart, you're going to reach their hearts. If you talk with your life, you're going to reach their lives."

You can put these words can be put into practice immediately. Bring your group together, and in front of everyone, make a personal commitment. Promise to invest time, attention, energy, personal contact, and funding (if that is appropriate). Be specific. This isn't a pep talk or a moment in the limelight. Your group deserves to know exactly how invested you are.

Now go around the room and ask each person to make his or her own commitment. Ask what they are willing to invest. When everyone has done so, you have a working plan for action. As progress is being made, follow upon everyone's commitment. Carry through with all the resources you promised to invest. Recall that only 20 percent of people in the workplace report that their boss is willing to invest in a relationship with them. Nothing is more important if you want to recruit others to act.

Make sure that you keep the group abreast of every step of progress along the way to your goal. Make sure everyone realizes that you value feedback. And make sure that no one is left out of the loop.

RIGHT ACTION IN EVERY SITUATION

If you are aware, every situation will tell you which path is right and which is wrong. Each of the seven situations that we've been discussing calls for its own kind of action.

1. Protector: Your role is crisis manager. As a role model, you show confidence and strength. You walk the walk by going to the center of the crisis and remaining there as long as it takes. You look for constant feedback as to how the crisis is shifting. Your persistence ensures that every aspect of the crisis is being attended to, overlooking no foreseeable possibilities. When the crisis is past, your whole team celebrates by embracing those who were saved from threat, bringing them to a feeling of safety, and releasing the tension and stress that every crisis creates.

2. Achiever: Your role is motivator. As a role model, you are the winner, the one who competes successfully. You walk the walk by bringing tangible rewards to the whole group, not just yourself. You look for stories of success, but you are also alert to the things people are less willing to share: their doubts and obstacles that block the way to success. You persist in the face of competition and setbacks, which are inevitable. You encourage the group to realize that every challenge can be met. When success is finally achieved, you celebrate by sharing the credit and the rewards, pointing out each person's unique contribution and allowing exultation to have its day.

3. Team Builder: Your role is negotiator. As a role model, you convince the group that you support shared goals instead of rivalries and factions. You walk the walk by being fair and just, showing no favoritism. The feedback you look for is agreement. Disagreement is inevitable, and you remain alert for potential cracks in the group so that you can heal them before they turn into rifts. You persist by reconciling differences, even though each party may be stubborn and stuck in its own position. When you have achieved group unity, you celebrate by relaxing as a group outside work, finding an activity that everyone can enjoy together. Let the group feel its solidarity without the pressure of a deadline to meet.

4. Nurturer: Your role is counselor. As a role model, you express sympathy and understanding to anyone who comes to you in trouble or need. You walk the walk by never judging; your empathy extends to everyone, because everyone goes through tough times. The feedback you look for is any sign that people feel listened to and understood. On the other hand, you are also alert to anyone who looks disengaged or alienated from the group. You persist by following up with the people who need you, keeping tabs on how they are doing, and committing yourself to building a real relationship. Celebration takes place one person at a time, when you are able to share another's intimate joys and steps toward healing.

5. Innovator: Your role is catalyst. As a role model, you encourage new ideas and show that you are comfortable with the unknown—in fact, it excites you. You walk the walk by creating a space for creativity to flourish, and by nurturing the first sprouts of a promising discovery. The feedback you are looking for is any sign of a breakthrough. You keep your antennae out for signs of progress, steering the group away from dead ends and unpromising lines of inquiry. When the breakthrough has been made, you celebrate by appreciating as a group the beauty and wonder of being pioneers.

6. Transformer: Your role is inspirer. As a role model, you exemplify a higher calling, and your voice amplifies the inner voice that calls every person to be transformed. You walk the walk by upholding the values you preach.

The feedback you look for is any sign of an internal shift in your group—a group that could be as large as a whole society. You are alert to evidence that people are acting out of their better natures. You persist by showing compassion, no matter how often your people backslide or show weakness. The celebrations you lead are often rituals of thanks and worship. The group is drawn together as children of a higher power.

7. Sage and seer: Your role is pure light. You have reached the highest state of awareness. As a role model, you are saintly, a purified soul. You walk the walk by emanating the very qualities of Being—love, truth, peace, and a deep knowingness. What you do is almost irrelevant. Your feedback is anything and everything: the sage accepts that each person is following a unique path that must be honored. You persist by understanding human nature in any guise. You celebrate by uniting with the One, the field of pure being that is the source of everything. Others celebrate by absorbing your inner peace and joy.

Because human nature is complicated, it is up to you to identify the role you need to play. If you are prepared at the level of deepest awareness, every role is open to you. The most powerful leaders in history, such as Gandhi, Churchill, and Lincoln, fulfilled all seven roles, which is the key to their greatness.

Every situation calls for a flexible response, but some values cannot be compromised if you are to play your role successfully. These values come from within. Without them, a leader will be torn by the conflicts bombarding him from every side. Don't present such a strong ego that you won't bend; rather, to resolve a problem, know where it is desirable to bend and where it isn't.

What Isn't Negotiable

Protector: I won't give up being centered. If I don't feel strong and secure inside, I can't manage the crisis at hand.

Achiever: I won't give up my self-confidence. If I don't feel that I will succeed, I can't motivate others to succeed.

Team Builder: I won't give up my impartiality. If I don't treat everyone fairly, I can't persuade others to settle their differences.

Nurturer: I won't give up my insight. If I can't see beneath the surface to discover how people really feel, they won't feel understood.

Innovator: I won't give up my curiosity. If I am not open to all possibilities, I can't lead the way to new discoveries.

Transformer: I won't give up my moral vision. If I am not inspired, I can't lead others to a higher way of life.

Sage and Seer: I am unique because there is nothing I won't give up. The universe brings all things and takes them back again. Being connected to the cycle of creation and destruction, I encompass both.

These inner values will be your support in the most difficult situations. You won't negotiate over them because they are part of you. To give them up would be like tearing yourself down. The surest way to know that you truly fit the role you are playing is to be totally secure about where you will compromise and where you won't.

ACT SMART

Even as you act out your role, there are some specific keys to successful action. Remember, it's not how well you fit your part that will determine your greatness as a leader. The ultimate test is right action, the kind that is clear and decisive and leads to the intended result. Imagine you are in charge of handling an emergency like Hurricane Katrina or a massive oil spill. As the first person on the scene with your team, you must take decisive action in the shortest period of time. Three routes are open to you.

A: You set up a chain of command with Washington. Your handbook contains approved procedures for dealing with this kind of emergency. Even though there is chaos everywhere, you await orders from above. You have a job to do, but there's a right way to do it. By looking out for yourself and your job, you aren't doing wrong: you are being loyal to the powers who stand over you.

B: You keep on the go, assessing the emergency from

the field. You race to the worst damage spots in order to bring help where it is most needed. You check in with Washington regularly, but you take on major responsibility yourself. This is your show, however it turns out. Like a general commanding troops in the field, you give orders decisively, expecting them to be obeyed. Thanks to the confidence that higher-ups place in you, you never lose control over the situation.

C: You visit the scene of destruction daily, but otherwise you stay put. You delegate authority with the understanding that your lieutenants must be willing to make some tough decisions on their own. Every step of the way you assess who is best to solve a given problem. You improvise in your methods. You don't hesitate to take risks, because you know that emergencies call for the greatest accomplishments, and those don't come without risk. You set nearly impossible goals and deadlines, yet somehow they get met.

These three styles of action should seem very familiar. In an age of continuous media coverage, the public sees how emergencies are handled. The first kind of leader (a team player who never breaks the rules) can be instantly separated from the second kind of leader (who responds with intense personal commitment and monitors the crisis on the ground himself). But the third kind of leader isn't so easily spotted, because he takes action that is unpredictable and spontaneous. He does more on the inside than on the outside. He can be extremely involved or seemingly detached as his inner guidance tells him to be.

This kind of leader has consciously chosen how he will act. Whatever the emergency, he works from a foundation of awareness. His actions are the smartest of the three because he reaches beyond his own perspective, trying to grasp the emergency from as many viewpoints as possible, then absorbing the whole picture. Intelligence is a quality of consciousness. It is personal, insofar as one person may be more intelligent than another. But that is a limited distinction. A great leader doesn't have to possess the highest IQ in the group. His talent is to pool as much intelligence as possible, reaching in all directions.

We can describe his methods using the acronym SMART, which applies to every leadership situation, not just crises and emergencies. No matter what role you play, you can act smart.

• S—Stretch the group to exceed its grasp so that people see that a vision is at work and can be realized. Avoid repetition and routine.

• M—Measure every step toward achieving the goal. Measurable goals are tangible, visible. Information is shared and known by the whole group. Avoid being imprecise and vague.

• A—Agreement should be the basis of decisions. Move forward with the agreement of everyone who is participating. Avoid unilateral actions and arbitrary rules.

• R—Record the progress being made. Let everyone know that he or she is part of an unfolding story, a journey. Avoid random, meaningless procedures.

• T—Time limits should be set for the goal. These limits are not constraints; they free each member to find his or her own personal rhythm while remaining aware of a definite end date. Avoid open-ended schedules.

By consciously deciding to act smart, you avoid two great pitfalls of inadequate leadership. The first is ego, the reliance on yourself as the only authority, the center of attention, the person who has to be right. The other pitfall is lack of outreach. Intelligence exists everywhere in the universe, in every cell of our bodies, and in all people. Therefore the most natural way to access this field is to widen your gaze—the farther you cast your net, the more you will know.

A great deal depends on taking right action instead of wrong action. The difference lies not in the uncertain future but in you and the authenticity of your vision. You are the source. With you and in you, the spark is ignited. Therefore your position is unique in the whole group. To ensure that you are truly acting from the soul, where all right action begins, keep asking yourself these questions:

> *Do your actions symbolize what the group is*
> *all about?*
> *Do you carry out the action demanded by your vision?*
> *Is your action responsive to the needs being expressed?*
> *Are you doing what you promised everyone you*
> *would do?*
> *Are you moving aside the resistance that lies in the*
> *way of every intention?*
> *Are you affirming the joy and fulfillment that is the*
> *result of successful action?*

THE SPIRITUAL SIDE OF DOING

The classic sign that a person is leading from the soul is that she stops struggling and lets life unfold. In Eastern spiritual traditions this approach is sometimes called "nondoing," which is considered more powerful than doing. You can actually accomplish more with less when you practice nondoing. It is very far from doing nothing. Imagine that you are at a sports event, such as a football or baseball game. An exciting moment has arrived—a last-minute pass for a touchdown or a high fly ball sailing for the fence. On the field the receiver or the outfielder knows that everything depends on him. His body and mind are at peak alertness. Events are moving so swiftly that the difference between success and failure is a matter of split seconds.

In such situations, athletes report that they sometimes go into "the zone." Despite the tenseness of the moment, they feel extremely relaxed. The deafening noise of the crowds disappears, replaced by silence. The player feels calm and knows, with total certainty, that he will catch the ball. Sometimes he feels as if he is witnessing his actions, as if he is completely uninvolved and the ball is destined to arrive at the exact place in space and time. Spectators in the stands see no sign that the player is in the zone. The externals remain the same, but the internal experience is dramatically transformed. Struggle has turned into allowing. Doing has crossed an invisible line to become nondoing.

Being in the zone is unpredictable, but you can learn to

set the stage for it. Sometimes we push our bodies into extreme effort, but most of the time we stand aside and let the body do what it does. The heart, lungs, kidney, and brain don't operate less efficiently when we step aside. In fact, if you worry about your blood pressure, it is likely to go up. If you try to force yourself to remember a word, it is less likely to appear. There's a fine balance between letting the body's intelligence operate on its own and taking control. The Eastern teaching about nondoing holds that just as you can step aside from controlling your body, you can step aside from controlling your life. Your life will still work very well if you don't control it. It will flow, unfold, grow, and evolve. By allowing, you become the witness to what your soul wants, and because you trust your soul, what it wants meshes perfectly with what you want. When that fusion takes place, being in the zone isn't a matter of magical moments on the playing field. It's a way of life.

A successful visionary has reached the stage where non-doing is natural. Having experienced what it's like to let life unfold on its own, she possesses a great advantage. Her approach to leadership can avoid the struggle, worry, stress, and control that brings down so many cherished projects. Letting your soul do the work is the most efficient way to lead as well as the most spiritual. In particular, four principles operate from the soul level:

> *Consciousness has organizing power.*
> *Consciousness makes quantum leaps of creativity.*
> *Consciousness moves naturally in the direction of growth.*
> *Consciousness creates order out of disorder.*

Now instead of using the word *consciousness,* substitute the word *I.* These four principles exist through you. You activate them. This is the true meaning of acting as the soul of the group. Allowing your soul to act through you opens a path so that the people you work with can activate their own souls. However, when you struggle, worry, and try to be in control, you block the soul's influence. A successful visionary takes practical steps to ensure that that doesn't happen. For each of the four principles there are definite do's and don'ts.

Consciousness has organizing power.

Do: Let events fall into place. When something gets stuck, first adopt a wait-and-see attitude. Act when you feel clear and centered. Allow other people to follow their own natural way of doing things. Tolerate diverse approaches. Trust that your soul has a plan, and even if you can't see it completely, know that everything will unfold as it is meant to.

Don't: Plan excessively. When you make a plan, leave room for changes. Don't impose one right way of doing things. Don't try to nail down every detail in advance. Don't worry about the unknown—it contains the most creative solutions. Don't take on the burden of knowing everything in advance. When in doubt, don't overthink, and don't rush in to control things.

Consciousness makes quantum leaps of creativity.

Do: Expect the unexpected, and be comfortable with it. Ask yourself for new solutions, and then let go so they have time to gestate within you. Trust that there is always an answer. Look beyond the level of the problem: the solution is almost always at another level. Rely on your intuition. Follow hunches, and enjoy where they lead you—chance encounters are often the most productive. Keep in contact with people whose minds work very differently from yours, and pay attention to what they say from their unique viewpoint. Keep a journal of your brainstorms, and just as helpfully, let your imagination run wild in your journal.

Don't: Keep repeating the same failed approach. Doing more of what didn't work in the first place won't take you where you want to go. Don't talk only to those who already agree with you. Don't be closed to crazy ideas and outlandish dreams—they might lead to unexpected breakthroughs. Don't forget that you are the source of infinite creativity, waiting to be tapped.

Consciousness moves in the direction of growth.

Do: Trust that growth is endless, since awareness has no limits. Treat life as a classroom where every day is the first day of school. If you have a choice, be last in the class ahead of you rather than first in the class behind you. Aim for the highest achievement, and be guided step by step from the core of your being. To activate growth, add some fertilizer in the form of energy, attention, and passion.

Don't: Think you've reached the end. There's always another step of evolution waiting for you. Don't assume that you know the whole story—there's always another page to turn. Don't set your sights low. Don't settle for good enough.

Consciousness creates order out of disorder.

Do: Trust that everything has a reason. Look for that reason rather than focusing on the chaos. Keep your mind open to the bigger picture that is emerging. Keep in touch with the meaning and purpose of your work. Remind yourself of the greater good behind every day's effort. As new levels of success unfold, aim even higher. There is infinite orderliness in Nature, therefore any order of complexity can be effortlessly arranged.

Don't: struggle against disorder. Creation uses disorder to bring about new answers. Don't impose an arbitrary or rigid kind of organization. The order imposed by the mind is ugly compared to the beautiful order that Nature unfolds. Don't add to the stress of the situation. Don't put up resistance to change just because you feel uncomfortable: be open to the new order that wants to emerge.

If you adopt these principles, you will discover that allowing has tremendous power. Instead of trying to figure out every step of your personal journey, you can let your soul reveal what is needed next. What is needed next cannot be predicted. Do you know the day and hour of your next brilliant idea? Again, this isn't the same as doing nothing. Your soul may tell you to jump into action; it may tell you to wait and see, or anything in between. The point is that consciousness flows where it is needed. The soul sends the message that suits the moment.

Behind the mystery of nondoing lies a simple, profound truth: your soul wants to take care of you completely. All true leaders embody this truth, because in their heart of hearts leaders want to serve. Their greatest fulfillment lies in bringing fulfillment to others. Therefore doing and nondoing, although they sound like opposites, actually merge. Nondoing brings you close to your soul. From that level, everything you do serves the highest purpose of life, the well-being of the group, and your own personal mission.

The Lessons of Doing

- Leading from the soul means doing what is right from the level of being. You actions are grounded in awareness. Coming from a deep level, your actions are supported by the universe.
- The role a leader plays depends upon the situation and its needs. If your awareness is expanded, you can fill all seven roles that match the seven basic situations that life brings.
- In spiritual terms the highest form of doing is

nondoing, or allowing. This is action that comes directly from the soul. In the state of nondoing you witness the unfolding of your being as it directs every step that leads you to your highest goals.

WHAT TO DO TODAY

As a leader you will be judged by your actions, and the step that precedes every action is decision making. You can increase your chance of making the right decision by being more aware. A decision that takes you in the right direction gives rise to a different feeling, a different atmosphere, and a different sense of other people from one that is wrong. This pertains while the decision is being made. If you tune in to how the process is going, you will become aware of the difference.

Decisions that turn out to be successful have certain features in common. Today if you find yourself having to make a critical decision, or even if you are contemplating one in the near future, ask yourself a few simple questions:

> *Does this decision feel right?*
> *Is it fair and honest?*
> *Can I trust what I'm being told?*
> *Where's the catch?*
> *Am I in over my head?*

If you look at the really bad decisions in your past, you'll see that you didn't ask or answer these questions properly. Somewhere in the decision-making process, you began to fool yourself—as countless others have done before you, at every level of leadership. You fell for illusion instead of reality because you became disconnected from your true self, the core of your personal values and purpose. This doesn't have to happen again.

The environment that surrounds good decision making has its own set of factors to indicate that you are in tune with your soul. Look over the following list and see if your current decisions, whether large or small, are being supported from the level of being.

20 ELEMENTS OF RIGHT DECISIONS

1. You are optimistic.
2. You don't indulge in wishful thinking.
3. You are not obsessively worrying about what can go wrong.
4. You can weigh the risks without undue fear.
5. You aren't blaming anyone for past mistakes.
6. You don't feel the need to ask for repeated reassurance.
7. You want the group to do what is best for everyone.
8. You assess criticism with detachment and fairness.
9. You decide to take reasonable risks.
10. You trust that there is always a solution waiting to present itself.
11. You encourage independent thinking.
12. You don't obsess over minute details.

13. You listen to the broadest range of people.
14. You realize the best way to go is unique to each situation.
15. You offer honest judgments without being brutal.
16. You focus without distraction.
17. You praise fully when someone gives positive input.
18. You set down reasonable rules that cause minimal constraint.
19. You are modest about your authority; you make no one feel small.
20. You participate from genuine enthusiasm.

If all or most of these elements are present, your decision making is highly conscious—you are tuned in. If few of these elements are present, your decision making is meeting with blocks and resistance. Until you become clearer inside, your choices will be too clouded to be reliable.

So today, if you can perceive that the environment isn't good, postpone making your decision until you have found the place inside you that is clear, coherent, calm, and self-aware. The secret, as always, is that every situation begins inside you and reflects where you are at this moment. Trust that your soul wants the best for you and that, with expanded awareness, you can unerringly find the right path. When the conditions "in here" are settled and clear, the results "out there" naturally follow suit.

Five

E = EMPOWERMENT

Empowerment is the fruit of successful action. Doing and having power go together, since without the power to sustain your vision through difficulties and resistance, your vision will wither away. This isn't ego empowerment, which is driven by the demands of "I, me, and mine"; you are empowering others at the same time as you empower yourself.

The belief that power isn't compatible with spirituality is misguided. At your source, there is a field of infinite possibilities. Packaged with every possibility is the path to achievement. Your soul unfolds both at the same time. Your power is validated by what you can manifest as reality.

There is a dark side to power, however, known as the shadow. This is where anger, fear, envy, greed, and aggression create problems for leaders, warping their good intentions and tarnishing their ideals. You must be aware of your shadow, and then you can defuse it by integrating the dark into the light. When you transcend the need for good and bad, for light and dark to war against each other, the power of the soul will be completely yours. This is the power of wholeness.

Every leader needs power, yet nothing brings more problems. Doing without it isn't an option. If you lack the power to reach your goals, your vision will remain inert. You have to be realistic about how power works before you can successfully empower yourself and then discover how to empower others, which is the greatest good a leader can do. The use of power is entangled with its misuse.

Seen through the lens of history, power follows certain principles, well illustrated by leaders ancient and modern.

• Power accumulates. The more a leader gets, the more will come to him.

• The powerful rise only to fall. The higher a leader climbs, the more inevitable is his downfall.

• Power corrupts. Leaders who start out to do good wind up doing evil.

• Power is exceptional. The ordinary person willingly or unwillingly surrenders his power to a handful of power-seekers and is left with none for himself.

These principles are acted out every day, and it doesn't take the huge stage of history to see them at work. As early as the sandbox, children can be seen dividing into bullies and victims, givers and takers, strong and meek. Psychologists tell us that gender roles are determined in early childhood: boys learn how to wield power, and girls learn how to appeal to power by being attractive and compliant. But even making simple statements about young children leads to controversy. No one wants to be told that she is among the meek rather than the strong, or that being a girl destines her to playing a lesser role than being a boy. Power has always been troubling.

Leading from the soul means resolving these troublesome issues by taking a conscious approach to them. With expanded awareness, one sees that the patterns of power are neither fixed nor inevitable. Each of the four principles can be reversed and transformed into something much more humane.

Power accumulates: To reverse this principle, renounce personal power for transpersonal power. Transpersonal power can be found in everyone. It is based on empathy, compassion, detachment, and going beyond ego to find your deeper identity.

The powerful rise only to fall: To reverse this principle, ground yourself in being, which is steady and ever-present. Its energy powers the universe from the level of the quantum field, the invisible starting point of all things visible. Here every possibility is equal. When you can bring out the fullest potential in any situation, your power will be steady, without the risk of rising too high or taking a fall.

Power corrupts: To reverse this principle, learn from your shadow and turn its negative influence into something positive. There is a dark side to every leadership role; when you are unconscious of it, the dark side leads to personal corruption. Yet the energies of the shadow, such as anger, resentment, selfishness, greed, and envy, are woven into life as a whole. They represent the destructive aspect in Nature, without which creation cannot emerge. Once you make creative use of the shadow, which is its ultimate purpose, power will not corrupt you.

Power is exceptional: To reverse this principle, empower others by showing them that they are equal to you. In reality, power is universal. The same energy, creativity, and orderliness are present in an atom and a galaxy, a one-celled bacterium and the human brain. We are misled by appearances and miss the hidden, invisible level from which power comes. If you share this knowledge, you can empower others to activate the source of power in themselves. Then everyone is exceptional, not just the few.

When you have reversed all four principles, you are fully empowered. Empowerment is not a desirable end in itself, however. Although being powerless brings many problems, so does misusing power. You must forge a link between power and deeper values. We look around us and see a world where every kind of horror exists through tyranny, oppression, military force, and persecution of the weak. You can be a force to counter these troubles, but you have to be willing to confront power consciously, here and now.

PERSONAL OR TRANSPERSONAL?

The first principle we want to reverse is "power accumulates." For many leaders this poses a terrible temptation, because they are motivated by the need to be in charge, to control, to make every decision. Their vision may be benign—all tyrants tell themselves that they are serving the greater good—but being good or bad isn't really the issue. The issue is ego, which needs no excuse to gain more for itself. When "I, me, and mine" dominates, the leader identifies with position and status. Ego is insecure by nature, so it is impossible to be strong without making others weak. As the ego sees it, every contest has winners and losers, and if glory goes to the winner, shame comes to the loser.

Before ego can undermine you, ground yourself in transpersonal power. Transpersonal power isn't ego-based. It exists equally in everyone. *Transpersonal* literally means "beyond the personal," or "belonging to everyone." By drawing on universal qualities, you as a leader become first among equals. You are made first by embodying more of what everyone desires. Instead of being a threat, your power inspires others. You are exercising transpersonal power when you bring to others the things most universally desired. When thousands of people were asked what they most wanted from a leader, four desires topped the list: trust, compassion, stability, and hope. When your power comes from supplying these things, it has shifted from personal to transpersonal.

Trust: People want to trust their leaders, to be secure in the knowledge that they will not be manipulated and misled. Trust is an invisible bond. It says, "I can't see what you are doing. I can't control or check up on you. But that doesn't matter. My trust is enough." People must trust that higher-ups are competent and can be counted on not to break their word.

By being open with everyone, keeping no secrets, describing situations realistically, and providing evidence that you are taking practical steps to meet any challenge, you show that as a leader you can be trusted with power. A leader who is not to be trusted does the opposite: she is obsessed with secrecy and closing down leaks. She reminds the group that she is to be feared. She tells the story that will keep her in power rather than the story that is true.

The tools for building trust are honesty, candor, and competence.

Compassion: Compassion makes people feel cared for. It draws out everyone's common humanity and keeps a group from disintegrating. When difficulties arise, there is always a pull between "every man for himself" and "we have to stick together." Empathy wars with selfishness. A leader can settle this conflict through compassion, a word that means "suffering with." By showing that you feel everyone's pain, you inspire the group to draw together. Each is motivated to feel for the person next to him. When you know what it feels like to walk in someone else's shoes, there is no choice but respect.

Empathy isn't only about pain. You feel the joy of another person's life as well. Their successes are yours and vice versa. When you feel empathy, you close the gap that separates isolated individuals. Compassion may seem like a passive or "soft" attitude, but it translates into powerful loyalties. Mutual help is offered. Mutual gratitude is felt. Once people are grateful for the things they share, the boundary has been crossed from personal to transpersonal.

The tools for building compassion are empathy, respect, and gratitude.

Stability: The soul is peaceful, calm, and capable of adapting to any kind of change. These are transpersonal qualities, built into the deepest level of our being. As a leader, you must project these qualities in order to make others feel stable. Instability embodies uncertainty. It makes people feel that the ground beneath their feet is crumbling. Reason can easily give way to panic (which is why markets can topple a bank simply on the rumor of insufficient funds).

The most basic aspect of stability is survival. It begins with knowing that you are going to be paid for your work. (Gallup researchers have found that workers who believe in the financial stability of their company are nine times more likely to be engaged in their work.) But as a leader you are asked to provide a deeper sense of stability. When the circumstances get dicey, uncertainty becomes a powerful stress. Everyone feels very alone. To counter the isolation, a leader offers support. The promise "I'll always be here for you" is carried out in actions. To counter uncertainty, he is always reliable. He won't suddenly turn and look out only for himself. By his presence, such a leader has a calming influence; he serves as a haven in the storm, which allows people to find this same quality in themselves. Then leadership has crossed over from the personal to the transpersonal.

The tools for building stability are reliability, support, and peace.

Hope: Hope is intangible because it rests upon belief. Your role is to be believer-in-chief. You hold out hope for a better future than anyone else can see. Hopelessness is the most tragic turn that life can take, depriving people of a vision for their future. The suffering of today blights hope for tomorrow. But at the soul level the future is always open because unseen possibilities can always awaken. (When Gallup pollsters asked workers if their leaders made them feel encouraged about the future, 69 percent of those who said yes were also engaged in their work; only 1 percent of those who said no were engaged.)

As a leader you must keep the horizon full of promise. Promise provides power. Instinctively people realize this, and they cling to hope even when a crisis seems beyond repair. In the worst storms, hope is the flickering candle that a leader cannot allow to be extinguished.

To give another person hope, a leader's inspirational words are only the beginning. When we lose hope, we become directionless. Therefore a leader must provide clear direction, a definite step-by-step plan. Eventually people can be allowed to provide their own direction, which in itself will be a sign of hope, but until then you must provide it. Work hands on to guide the group through all the recovery efforts that follow an immediate crisis. Also, respect the weakened position that people find themselves in. Guide them past shame and guilt. Providing guidance means holding out the values that need to be restored, such as self-confidence, competence, and worthiness. Through your showing that you see these values in others, they will begin to see them in themselves. When you show others a concrete way to move forward, you give them a reason to have faith. That's proof that they have crossed over to the transpersonal, since faith is based on belief in a higher power, however you choose to define it.

The tools for building hope are direction, guidance, and faith.

POWER MADE PERMANENT

The second principle that needs to be reversed is "the powerful rise only to fall." The reasons for taking a fall are many. Power-hungry people make enemies who want to bring them down. They are insecure to begin with, and they engineer their own fall by dirty deeds and secretive manipulation. The ego is so insecure that it fails to see the mistakes it is making, intent as it is on building an oversized self-image that is bound to implode. But in terms of the soul, these are all secondary causes. In spiritual terms, to seek power is to lose it, because what you seek you already are. The great Bengali poet Rabindranath Tagore put this truth beautifully when he wrote, "Those who seek, knock at the gate. Those who love find it open." Love is an aspect of being, and when you act from being, the power you draw on is limitless because it comes from the source. This kind of power is steady. It doesn't rise or fall. Therefore if you depend upon it, you don't have to climb to the top to achieve power.

Imagine three leaders who want to achieve the same thing: starting a company, building a bridge, or popularizing a new idea or invention. Leader A is a doer. He makes connections with people who can help him achieve his goal. He hires a good team; he knows how to get others as excited as he is about the project. His day is filled with appointments and decisions. At the hub of activity, he becomes the linchpin. All decisions come through him. In short order he makes himself indispensable. This kind of power can be very effective, but it is also the most insecure. For every success, there are many people who fail to achieve along this path. Someone stronger or more charismatic might beat them out. They may not be able to sustain the demands for energy and time that mount up, eventually swallowing up everything. Power based on doing can be taken from you, and even when it isn't, every day brings a confrontation with uncertainty, since the world is full of risks.

Leader B is a thinker rather than a doer. He might be the power behind the throne, or the source of ideas who leaves the practical side of the project to others. In either role, his strength is that he can analyze. He weighs options, observes other people, and comes to conclusions rationally. He isn't tossed around by the rough-and-tumble of everyday pressures. He is more distant but also more isolated. The danger for such a leader is that personal bonds can weaken. Loyal followers who admire his ideas tend to drift away when better ideas come along. Still, the leader who thinks is more secure than the doer, because his mind sustains him. He is grounded at a deeper level than personal loyalties, connections, and the daily grind of making things happen.

Leader C is grounded in being. He isn't invested in either doing or thinking. Every day his existence is focused on keeping to the right path, wherever it leads. He is spared the constant demands for energy that the doer must keep up with; he is also spared the isolation of the thinker, who needs doers to bring his ideas into the real world. To others around him, the leader who is grounded in being often seems mysterious. They can't quite figure out how he maintains his calm in a crisis and how he decides when to act, because sometimes he allows events to unfold while at other times he leaps into action. Such a leader makes for a successful visionary because he is selfless enough to permit his soul to guide him. He is immune to taking a fall because he has no desire to climb to the top. His sole purpose is to watch his vision unfold, therefore his path is one of expansion, not rising.

To become this kind of leader, your actions must be organized around the expansion of consciousness. In previous chapters we've covered how to connect to the level of being. Now you need to participate in the infusion of being into everyday life. Naturally, this new way challenges your old ways. As you negotiate your way, being will create the change you want. There is no need to fight against your past conditioning and familiar habits. Instead, a natural shift takes place. To encourage that shift, here's a guide.

How to Encourage Your Being

Before making a decision, ask inside for guidance. Be patient and await an answer.

Act only when you feel calm and certain.

Trust that there is a right path.

Trust that you are connected to your being, which knows what to do at all times.

When you meet with resistance, inside or out, don't fight back. Do what it takes to resolve the resistance and turn it into acceptance. If resistance persists, distance yourself and give it time.

Be fully engaged, but at the same time cultivate detachment.

Know that you are greater than any result, good or bad.

Identify yourself with the bigger picture and not the minute details.

Believe that your awareness can expand without limitation. To say "I am the universe" isn't egocentric—it's the truth of our soul.

PURE POWER

The third principle that needs to be reversed is "power corrupts." If you believe that human nature is innately selfish and greedy, the corruption of power will seem inevitable. But perhaps the premise is wrong. If human nature isn't fixed, it is open to choice. You can choose not to abandon your ideals and keep true to our vision. The trick is to escape either/or thinking, because it's common to believe that either you are powerful or you are an idealist. The visionary doesn't have to be separate from the realist. At the level of being, your vision is united with the way to achieve that vision. If you can keep them united, power will serve idealism instead of corrupting it.

As we've seen, the dark side of human nature is called the shadow, the hidden area of the psyche where anger, fear, greed, envy, and violence are kept out of sight. When any leader turns soulless, the shadow has triumphed. The simplest and most basic question, "Who am I, really?" has stopped being asked. The shadow causes enormous problems; it's hard to think of a human misery that isn't rooted there. Whatever you haven't faced has power over you. You may set out to do nothing but good, but unless you become conscious of your shadow, the result will be denial. In a state of denial you will face all kinds of negative effects from the external world, but you will be ill equipped to defeat them. Negativity is defeated only when you can integrate it into the whole fabric of life. If you are caught up in separating good from evil, light from shadow, you may play the part of goodness, but somehow badness will always crop up to counter you. Leading from the soul means finding a way to fuse opposites so that you stand for life as a whole, not simply the bright side.

To begin with, be aware that every role you play as a leader has a specific shadow that matches it.

The **protector's shadow** is the temptation to become a tyrant. Instead of removing fear and threat, he promotes it. He wants to be told how much "the little people" need him. His self-importance leads him to excuse how he abuses others. To keep himself in power, he exaggerates the threats that exist and even invents imaginary rivals and enemies. The end, when it comes, is ugly and often violent as he is toppled against his will.

To counter the shadow: Be aware of any sign in yourself of authoritarianism, self-importance, uncontrolled anger, the need for flattery, and paranoia about threats and rivals. These are the seeds of the tyrant.

The **achiever**'s shadow is addiction to winning, fueled by the never-ending desire for more. Underneath, she has an even stronger fear of losing. This fear clouds her judgment. She begins to indulge in excessive risk taking—she is so addicted to winning that the next high always needs to be greater than the last. All proportion is lost, and with it the connection to others. Success now means more than family and friends. While claiming that she is still in control of herself, the achiever who has turned into an addict eventually takes one risk too many. Then she brings herself down and others with her.

To counter the shadow: Be aware of any sign in

yourself of turning encounters into win-lose situations, polishing your self-image, being ambitious at the cost of family and friends, and obsessing over competitors. These are the seeds of addiction to success.

The **team builder's shadow** is conformity, fueled by the fear of not belonging. Constantly attuned to the reactions of others, he cannot bear to make enemies and feels wounded by criticism. The conformist comes to epitomize the "tall poppy syndrome," punishing anyone who tries to stand out above the group. His need to placate everyone leads him to overlook footdraggers and time-servers. Instead of fostering cooperation, he fosters complacency. The end, when it comes, involves a smarter, more energized team-builder swallowing the conformist up.

To counter the shadow: Be aware of any sign in yourself of going along to get along, never making waves, acting against your conscience, and envying others for their special talents and abilities. These are the seeds of conformity.

The **nurturer's shadow** is judgment, fueled by the fear of not being good enough. This fear gets projected outward, making others wrong in order to feel right. Instead of empathizing with how other people feel, someone acting from judgment tells them what they should be feeling. As real connections dissolve, the failed nurturer falls back on pretense, a show of warmth and bonding. Secret biases must be hidden. She can't afford to let anyone know that she secretly judges them. The end, when it comes, arrives through the exposure of hypocrisy. The loving, fair, nonjudgmental nurturer has been leading a double life.

To counter the shadow: Be aware of any sign in yourself of hiding your prejudices instead of openly discussing them, showing favoritism, harboring secret motives, and pretending to be better than you are. These are the seeds of judgment.

The **innovator's shadow** is solipsism, fueled by fear of risks. Instead of being open to new ideas, he promotes his past achievements. His reputation looms large in his own mind. He craves recognition—ideally, everyone should honor him as a master of his craft. Beneath this show of self-centeredness, risk has taken its toll. To hide from his inability to take chances, the failed innovator stops peering into the unknown. The end, when it comes, finds him outmoded and behind the curve.

To counter the shadow: Be aware of any sign in yourself of smugness, jealousy, cravings for attention, insecurity about your reputation, and a reluctance to invest yourself in unproven ideas. These are the seeds of solipsism.

The **transformer's shadow** is despair, fueled by society's stubborn resistance to change. In place of hope, which every transformer must show, depression begins to gnaw its way in. The failed transformer finds herself personally wounded by setbacks. She grows ever more disappointed by the moral weakness of others, but her greatest disappointment is reserved for herself. Her cherished ideals are being tarnished; she throws herself against the barricades over and over without success. The end, when it comes, arrives not at the hands of reactionaries but when the crusade runs out of steam.

To counter the shadow: Be aware of any sign in

yourself of personal blame, guilt, cynicism, depression, and resignation that nothing will ever change. These are the seeds of despair.

The sage and seer don't have a shadow. They have uncovered their dark side and released themselves from it. Yet ironically, their liberation can make others suspicious. It's hard to believe that the sage isn't hiding some foible and that the seer hasn't got a blind spot. But criticism and even open attack don't faze the sage and seer. They accept every aspect of the human condition. There is no end to the sage's journey. He walks ahead, striving to turn suffering into joy. To him, the world's suffering is a mask for eternal bliss.

Once you become aware of your shadow, the next step is to defuse it. What doesn't work is to resist, fight, steel yourself, or go into denial. The shadow may feel like an enemy, but Nature brings about creation through destruction. The wholeness of life depends upon reconciling these two forces. In yourself, anger, fear, resentment, envy, and greed emerge as negative forces because they aren't integrated. "Good me" and "bad me" are at war. Until you disengage from the war, you have no recourse except struggle. The seeds of anger and fear will grow, and because they are flourishing out of sight, in the dark, they become more distanced from the light. Increasing isolation causes natural expressions of the destructive force to become renegades, randomly causing harm wherever they can.

To take the shadow beyond war and strife, make it your goal to integrate "bad me" into "good me." Your soul is beyond opposites. If you aim at the full integration of every aspect of yourself, you are doing exactly what your soul wants you to do.

Merging with Your Shadow

Be aware of feelings like anger, anxiety, envy, grief, and selfishness.

Acknowledge that these feelings are part of you.

Forgive yourself for having a shadow.

Take responsibility for what you feel. Don't project onto others, blame them, or take your negativity out on them.

Take a vow against any form of violence and aggression.

When you feel the emergence of a negative emotion, sit quietly and feel it in your body. Ask for the emotion to resolve itself, which means that you release it, taking whatever time is necessary.

Trust that all residues of fear, anger, grief, jealousy, and insecurity can be released. If you are able, seek help from a counselor, body worker, or other guide who is skilled in releasing old traumas and past wounds.

Resist the urge to push away or deny those feelings you judge against. If you force them to exist out of sight, they will only undermine you.

Don't keep secrets. Find someone with whom you can share anything, and then proceed, as appropriate, to bring "bad me" out for discussion.

Work on the shadow one piece at a time. It is much easier to dismantle a strongly negative aspect of yourself, such as uncontrollable fear, free-floating anxiety, a hair-trigger temper, or deep-seated resentment, than it is to confront it head on. These uncontrolled tendencies are pieced together by old beliefs, childhood experiences, unrevealed secrets, hidden guilt and shame, judgment against the self, influences in your surroundings (such as stress, domestic strife, continuing abuse, and failure at work), and a superstitious attachment to concepts like absolute evil or the devil. By addressing each piece one at a time, even the most powerful shadow energy can be defused.

EQUALITY OF POWER

The last principle that we need to reverse is "power is exceptional." There's no doubt that it feels good to feel special, and leaders who attain power cannot help but feel exceptional. That's not what needs reversing. Rather, we need to correct the ego's belief that only "I" am exceptional. The source of power is universal. Everyone contains infinite potential, and once it is released, the universe will either support it or not. As a leader, it's up to you to show the difference by guiding others onto a path that the universe will favor. You do this by the same means that you used on yourself, by connecting with the soul.

You cannot cajole, order, or force anyone else to reconnect with his soul, but you can inspire him to find his own motivation. We've already covered some of the most critical factors: acting as a role model, forming emotional bonds, building trust, compassion, stability, and hope. But until the people you lead are able to identify with what is best in themselves, they can't take the first step on their own path. Duplicating your path isn't a substitute. Ideally, you could have everyone in your group write out a mission statement based on her soul profile and personal vision. That is how we've been unfolding your own path. You can also take advantage of research, such as that performed by Gallup, which is used to identify each person's strengths in detail. In the Gallup model there are thirty-four specific strengths. If a team contains as many different strengths as possible, it improves their chance of success.

Taking this advice to heart, you can begin to share power by learning what to look for as a strength. Don't assume that people know their own strengths, but understand that until they discover them, they have no basis on which to build power. Look at each person you want to assess, and place him in three of the categories below. If you don't know the person well, you could choose only two categories, but it would be better to make a guess at the third and modify your assessment as you learn more.

21 Strengths to Build Upon

1. **Hardworking**. Has great stamina. Gets satisfaction from being busy and productive.

2. Very **active**. Is impatient to get beyond thinking into doing. Gets satisfaction by making a difference.

3. Good at getting people **into the flow**. Is now-oriented and highly adaptable. Gets satisfaction from showing others how to trust themselves and join in.

4. *Analytical.* Investigates every side of an issue. Is careful and trustworthy in his conclusions. Gets satisfaction from research.

5. Good at *planning*. Is good at arranging and organizing, but has a mind open to everyone's demands. Is honest and expects honesty in return. Gets satisfaction by pulling many elements together.

6. Naturally *communicative.* Can easily put thoughts into words and shines when making a presentation. Gets satisfaction from showing others the positive side of the situation, and the positive in themselves.

7. *Competitive.* Measures herself by how she's doing compared to others. Wants to be judged as the best. Gets satisfaction by winning, obviously, but also from measuring up to those she respects most.

8. Modestly *reliable.* Shows consistency in applying the rules but also abides by them. Good at treating others on an equal footing. Gets satisfaction from seeing that everyone gets the same respect.

9. *Deliberate* in making decisions. Is good at handling sensitive issues because he takes due weight of every factor. Foresees obstacles that lie ahead. Gets satisfaction from making sound judgments that reduce risk and takes the time to get safely from here to there.

10. Talented in *developing* human resources. Sees the potential in others and is patient about bringing it out step by step. Trusts that someone can do the job before others recognize that. Gets satisfaction from watching beginners start to blossom.

11. *Self-disciplined.* Thrives on routine and structure.

Never slides or lets herself off the hook. Gets satisfaction from feeling responsible.

12. **Empathetic.** Is good in difficult situations where others must deal with conflicting emotions. Is sought out when someone needs to share. Gets satisfaction from making others feel understood.

13. **Prioritizing.** With a strong focus, keeps projects on track. Can be trusted to know what is important. Cuts through incidental details and avoids detours. Gets satisfaction from moving efficiently toward the ultimate goal.

14. Good at **building consensus**. Is averse to conflict and wants to reconcile differences. Works by listening and showing others the value of listening. Is valuable in any negotiation. Gets satisfaction when all sides come to an agreement that is mutually beneficial.

15. Full of **ideas**. Easily makes connections between disparate things. Thrives on absorbing as many perspectives as possible. Is never at a loss for a new concept. Gets satisfaction from the sheer fascination of ideas.

16. **Expert.** Specializes in a narrow field and knows everything about it. Brings authority and is respected by peers. Gets satisfaction from mastering a branch of knowledge and expertise.

17. **Boosterish.** Is constantly in pursuit of excellence and gets others to outperform themselves. Feels nothing is good enough until it is superb. Gets satisfaction by bringing any project to the highest level of quality.

18. Endlessly **enthusiastic.** Naturally upbeat and positive, she can make others share her enthusiasm without resentment or feeling coerced. Good at keeping up morale.

Gets satisfaction from making others see the bright side and believing in it.

19. *Loyal,* devoted, friendly. Is easy to relate to and also work beside. Others have confidence that he will always look out for them. Is willing to invest time and energy in relationships. Gets satisfaction from the bonds of sincere friendship.

20. The *fixer* puts out fires and solves problems. She restores hope and stabilizes situations that are falling apart. Unfazed by problems and is open to meeting needs. Gets satisfaction from doing the impossible.

21. Charming and *persuasive.* Is able to woo others to her way of thinking. Welcomes meeting new people. Is unfazed by difficult people. Others naturally open up to her and share information, even when they first meet. Gets satisfaction from breaking the ice and making a personal connection.

Once you gain insight into someone else's strengths, you can help him find his own path to empowerment. To begin with, tell him what you see and discuss his own sense of what he's strong at. If you are in a position to assign tasks, use his strengths as a guide. Even if you aren't assigning a task, keep in mind what everyone's strengths are. This will enable you to seek the right input from each person.

If a single theme runs through empowerment, it's the belief that all people have an equal right to power. Each of us is a complete person reflecting the wholeness of our soul. We may be hiding from our completeness, deliberately or not. Instead of relishing how multidimensional we are, most of us have become resigned to a narrow slice of life. Empowerment is about expanding expectations by revealing that all the negative assumptions about power don't have to be true. Power isn't something you grab; it's the infinite energy, intelligence, and creativity of the soul that wants to express itself through you. When you understand that everyone is the expression of a soul, you as a leader find joy in helping each individual uncover that truth. The highest spiritual lesson about power that I've ever read comes from Tagore: "Power said to the world, 'You are mine.' Love said to the world, 'I am yours.' Love won."

The Lessons of Empowerment

• Leading from the soul means reversing the ways that power is misused. The guiding principle is to empower others every step of the way, as you empower yourself.

• Cross the boundary that separates personal power from transpersonal power. *Transpersonal* means "going beyond the individual." This is the kind of power that exists within everyone at the level of the soul.

• Treading the path to power begins by knowing your personal strengths and building on them. The same is true when you empower others. With the expansion of awareness, you express the wholeness of your soul. Then your strength comes from the level of being.

WHAT TO DO TODAY

Power becomes a problem when the ego tries to co-opt it. Realize that power isn't about "I, me, and mine." Cultivate detachment in your role as a leader. People confuse feeling high with being powerful, but power derived from the soul is a combination of stillness and dynamism. It never runs out, even after the high is over. In detachment you can experience the surge of power without getting lost in it. You can move into any situation with a sense that everything you want is already inside you—this is a relaxed, assured state, and a place of power.

Today you can begin to practice detachment while still being fully engaged—that's the real trick, since a cool, aloof detachment is the same as indifference. But there's a model for detachment that comes naturally and is the opposite of indifference: play. When you watch a child at play, she's completely focused and engaged. The game is all-consuming. Distractions aren't a problem. The child is carefree and full of energy as long as the game doesn't turn serious and become about winning. The following exercise can bring you into this state of play as an adult.

When you wake up in the morning, allow yourself ten minutes in bed with your eyes closed. Visualize the day ahead. See the critical moments that hold important decisions or choices for you. See these situations turning out for the best. Don't tie yourself to a fixed scenario; just let your mind play with possibilities. Once you feel happy with a scene, go back and view it from another perspective.

Watch it turn out well, also, but along completely different lines. Return two or three times, playing with enough possibilities that you aren't stuck on only one—be as comfortable as you can with whatever your soul wants to bring to you.

When you are finished, leave aside your visualizations and meet the day with openness.

This exercise is about *lila* (pronounced "leelah"), or "the playfulness of creation," as it is known in Sanskrit. *Lila* is the way the soul operates, by enjoying the unfolding of every moment and turning "what is" into "what will be," not following a straight line or a predictable course but letting every ingredient contribute to something new. *Lila* is your natural state. You are falling out of it whenever the following is happening:

> *You invest your ego in winning.*
> *You hate losing.*
> *You have to be in control.*
> *You have to be right.*
> *You feel tense and uncomfortable.*
> *The stress is getting to you.*
> *Things get too serious.*
> *Nothing feels like fun.*

To truly play, you must become aware of these warning signs and do something about them. Every situation is different, but the feeling of play can always be recaptured if you listen inside and respect the truth that creativity is meant to be carefree. I'm not talking about forced jolliness, or mischief, or turning everything into a game. We all know what it's like to be innocent and carefree, a state that the soul never leaves. This is playfulness of the spirit.

If you keep up the exercise just described, you will begin to be less stuck on the need for control and a narrow fixity on which outcome is best. Every day is a new world, but we inhabit it as people who don't know how to be new. Detachment, in its purest form, is the willingness to renew yourself by letting go of old conditioning. In complete openness you let the new flood through you, and then you will become as playful as creation itself.

Six

R = RESPONSIBILITY

Leading from the soul means taking responsibility for more than the group's needs. It means having concern for everyone's personal growth. This responsibility begins with your own evolution. In eight areas of your life you have the power to be guided by your soul: thoughts, emotions, perception, personal relationships, social role, environment, speech, and the body. In all of these areas your behavior affects the people you lead. If you evolve, so will they.

Leading from the soul means that evolution is your top priority. You never act in such a way as to lower the self-esteem of others. You examine your underlying beliefs and modify them as new opportunities for growth reveal themselves. Because evolution is an unstoppable force in the universe, you draw upon invisible powers. Therefore being responsible is no longer a burden. It rests lightly on you as long as you continue to grow.

Every leader takes on responsibilities, but if you lead from the soul, you have a different perspective. You take responsibility for your evolution and the evolution of those around you. You've chosen to start out with a vision. In order to fulfill it, you walk a path that is about much more than external success. The inner person is growing every step of the way. The group is having higher needs fulfilled. So how do you equip yourself to keep evolving? Personal commitment plays a part, but to what do you commit? Once this question is answered, you'll know what your responsibilities actually are from day to day.

Your soul doesn't make any demands, because it isn't involved in activity. It functions as your source, the silent ground of your existence. Therefore your responsibility arises only when you have to act, think, and feel. Seeds are forever sprouting in silence. Each seed is a possibility arising from the field of infinite possibilities. A seed may sprout as your next thought. Your responsibility, then, is to make your next thought evolutionary—it should promote growth and progress. But a possibility doesn't always manifest as a thought. It could be a sensation, an action, or a word. Possibilities encompass every aspect of life. Your soul is capable of giving you anything you want, but the other side of the bargain is that you are responsible for what you ask for.

Knowing what to ask for can be quite subtle. However beautiful and inspiring your overall vision, there are thousands of details that must be worked out on a daily basis. A leader may be dedicated to building world peace or to working for a sustainable economy or to finding an alternative to fossil fuels. In comparison to such lofty goals, it seems petty to consider the next word you are about to say, or the next sensation you will feel in your body. But these are part of the fabric of life, and if they don't evolve, your vision won't evolve, either. The fabric of life is incredibly complex and interwoven, but we can find eight main strands, each with its own set of responsibilities. The joy of looking at the subject from this perspective is that you will be taking on responsibility not as a burden but as a way of nurturing yourself. Ask yourself one question—"Will I evolve by doing this?"—and if the answer is yes, accept the responsibility for your choice.

A leader's responsibilities can be divided into the following eight areas: I am responsible for what I think; I am responsible for how I feel; I am responsible for how I perceive the world; I am responsible for my relationships; I am responsible for my role in society; I am responsible for my immediate environment; I am responsible for my speech; I am responsible for my body. Now let's take a look at each of these in more detail.

I AM RESPONSIBLE FOR WHAT I THINK.

This is the field of cognition, which is much broader than rational thoughts: it also covers insight, intuition, "gut feelings," and creative impulses. Because they come to us spontaneously, we tend to accept that thoughts roam the mind at will. If that's true, how can we be responsible for mental impulses as they come and go? After all, you don't know what your next idea or hunch will be. But thoughts come in patterns; you have habits of thinking. These you can take responsibility for. Promote the good habits and avoid the bad ones. Successful leaders have learned to do both, often without knowing it (although a good percentage had to train their minds to meet the demands of being a leader).

GOOD MENTAL HABITS

Think clearly and concisely.

Weed out prejudices and personal biases.

Examine your assumptions to make sure they aren't secondhand or unproved.

Explore every thought in depth.

Pay attention to subtle impulses, focusing on them until they expand and unfold.

See each thought without judging or dismissing it prematurely.

Walk around and see your thought from several angles.

Be sure you aren't influenced too much by stress, emotion, or the heat of the moment.

Be above the drama of the situation.

Each of these points is something you can take responsibility for. Left to itself, the untended mind is neither clear nor concise. It needs to be trained to prune away repetition. In place of fuzzy, vague thinking, you shape your thoughts clearly, wording them concisely. The same attention is needed for all the other points. Unless we pay attention, prejudice creeps into our thinking automatically—that's the nature of habit, to reappear on its own. Time and again you have to pull up and say, "This isn't what I want to think. It's just old conditioning from the past, a stale repetition of what I used to think."

With cognition, your overall responsibility is to be self-aware. Only you can spot the effect that emotions and stress are having. No outside perspective can substitute for yours, even though trusted advisers can bring you to your senses by pointing out where you've lost clarity. Notice that two things are not on the list: organization and discipline. Some leaders owe their success to having a highly organized and disciplined mind. Examined closely, the need to force your mind into a discipline is like training a wild animal whose behavior you don't trust and whose wildness is undesirable. But as restless as the mind can be, it is also the source of spontaneous answers and solutions. Spontaneity requires freedom, and it's difficult for something to be free and disciplined at the same time.

Of course, your mind can't be left ragged and wild. Even the pure artist who cannot tolerate rules or boundaries will accept the discipline of learning his craft. You can take your cue from that: discipline your mind as a means of mastering your craft, but then let it be free. Otherwise you will dismiss too many "stray" thoughts that in fact have something to tell you. In the same vein, allow every subtle impulse of the mind—the vaguest hunch or intimation—to expand. This is particularly true when you feel a slight *uh-oh.* Under the pressure to agree with others, to find quick solutions, to be rid of a problem, we all jump to faulty conclusions. But the soul can't be fooled by externals, and when you feel, however subtly, that something isn't quite right, you must trust yourself. In fact, the subtler the *uh-oh,* the more it can be trusted.

I AM RESPONSIBLE FOR HOW I FEEL.

Even more than thoughts, feelings seem to come and go at will. Being spontaneous, emotions are often feared and distrusted. Nothing is more unwelcome to the mind than anxiety, and many a promising career has been undone by a bad temper. But we aren't talking about trying to control fear, anger, or any other emotion. (For one thing, programs for anger management and curing phobias have had mixed results at best; even the promising field of positive psychology, which sets out to reframe negativity in a positive way, remains largely unsupported by research.) But like thoughts, feelings fall into patterns, and by being aware of those patterns, you can take responsibility for changing them.

A feeling is a response that seems to happen suddenly and automatically. If you are afraid of spiders, the sight of one causes you to recoil in fear. If dirty dishes in the sink make you angry, you can't help being irritated when you walk into the kitchen after a meal and see that someone has neglected to wash up. But this apparent lack of choice is deceptive. Think of what happens when somebody throws a ball or a set of car keys at you. Even if you are caught off guard, either you will automatically put up your hand to catch it or you will move out of the way, mumbling "I can't catch things." These responses are opposites; somewhere in your life you either trained yourself to catch things or did not. Once trained, your response became ingrained, but you can always retrain it. You never lose freedom of choice, and fortunately the most advanced brain research indicates that new skills can be added to the brain over an entire lifetime.

You have trained yourself to feel a certain way and to avoid feeling another way. The trick, if you truly take responsibility, is to replace a trained feeling with openness. We all value positive feelings over negative ones, but if you train yourself never to be negative, you miss the fact that "negativity" is actually a judgment against the self. It's a label for "I am bad if I feel this way." We've all experienced the strain of being around people whose fixed smile and ever-present sunniness are unreal. Untraining your feelings means, first of all, noticing patterns. If you automatically respond by doubting, for example, or by pushing away new things, if you cringe in the face of change or of new people suddenly appearing in your life, step back and notice your feelings.

Having stepped back, wait and see. Quite often a first response will fade on its own. When it does, an open space appears, and in that space you can guide yourself to the feeling you want to have. Don't judge yourself. Let any feeling be what it is, but at the same time don't act on your fear, anger, resentment, envy, suspicion, or any other feeling that will promote stress in those around you. Feelings are yours until you project them into the world. It's your responsibility not to project what is harmful.

When you have learned to experience an open space where once you filled it with automatic reactions, something new appears. The soul begins to unfold its own feelings, which are always evolutionary. These aren't passing emotional events but a steady state of feeling. Silence, peace, and a calm sense of the self don't come and go. Once you contact them, they give rise to what Buddhism calls the four divine feelings: loving kindness, compassion, equanimity, and joy at the success of others. But it's not necessary to have a name for higher feelings. (Labeling them might even tempt you to train your mind to be "good.")

All the higher emotions take us out of our separate selves. It's the separate self that is trained to choose A over B, usually because the ego has decided that A contains a self-promoting benefit. Beyond the separate self there is a natural flow of feeling, and whatever reaction is appropriate will arise on its own. The soul always aims to give you the most evolutionary response possible, and that goes for feelings, too.

I AM RESPONSIBLE FOR HOW I PERCEIVE THE WORLD.

Perception, like thinking and feeling, seems to be automatic. If I perceive that the sky is blue, this doesn't seem like a choice, and you can only be responsible for what you choose. But once again, the absence of choice is deceptive. The one thing we do know is that possibility is never limited, so choice must always be present. By definition, a leader is someone who can see more possibilities than other people do. No matter what the hardship or setback seems to be, evolution is at play. You can adopt a style of seeing the world based on this principle: higher evolution is unstoppable.

The pioneering physicist Max Planck said, "When you change the way you look at things, the things that you look at will change." In a sense, this is how relativity works at the soul level. As you shift your perception, reality shifts to match. Therefore inner perception, which is your sense of self, is where reality begins. The more expanded your sense of self, the more possibilities are released from the level of the soul. You will never run out of possibilities unless you limit them yourself. The cause of limitation is belief. Negative beliefs act like censors. When faced with a set of possibilities, they say no to the first appearance of things that they judge too dangerous, wrong, bad, impossible, not worth having, or "not me." Your soul, on the other hand, wants to deny you nothing, but you will never know that if your beliefs are blocking all but a few possibilities. Every possibility that cannot see the light of day diminishes your future, doing its work invisibly and outside your awareness. What you need to do is become aware of these beliefs and then reverse them so that you hold evolutionary beliefs instead.

Beliefs That Block Your Future

I'm not good enough. I deserve less than other people.

Reversal: The more I evolve, the more I deserve. Since evolution is unlimited, so is my deserving.

Avoidance is a good way to postpone difficult decisions.

Reversal: Postponement is never a solution. It simply freezes the problem in place. If I solve the problem now, I have my whole future to enjoy the solution.

It doesn't help to focus on things that are wrong about me.

Reversal: Problems aren't bad. They are indications of where I need to grow. Beneath the difficulty lies a hidden ally. If I don't focus on my problems, I will miss the path of my own evolution.

The world is full of problems. What can just one person do?

Reversal: Evolution carries humanity forward one person at a time. I can become the change I want to see. When that happens, I contribute to the collective consciousness, and then everyone takes a step toward the critical mass required for change on the global level.

Change is too hard.

Reversal: Life is nothing but change. Every cell in my body changes constantly, as do my thoughts, feelings, and the events around me. The real point is that change can be conscious or unconscious. Simply by becoming more aware, I have become a powerful agent of change. There is no need to force anything, only to expand my awareness.

We are prisoners of random events and accidents outside our control.

Reversal: To be controlled by anything, including randomness, is to be a victim. Accidents are unknowable in advance. I have a choice to make the unknown either my friend or my enemy. As a friend, the unknown brings new life, new ideas, and new possibilities. I will focus on that and let go of the rest.

Everyone has enemies. I'd rather stay out of the fray and have as few enemies as possible.

Reversal: Enemy is just another word for obstacle. Whenever I meet an obstacle, my soul has put it there for a purpose and has provided a solution at the same time. I don't need to focus on what another person feels about me; my aim isn't to make friends with everyone. Instead, I am here to evolve and follow the path my soul is unfolding day by day.

I AM RESPONSIBLE FOR
MY RELATIONSHIPS.

Since relationships are two-sided, you can be responsible only for your part. But relating to someone else also brings a merging, so it isn't easy to separate out what your part is. A leader follows one general rule: when things are going well, praise the other person; when things aren't going well, be responsible for changing them. If you wait for another person to change things, or themselves, you may wait forever. You must arrive at self-sufficiency, which is the realization that you are enough. You never need another person to complete you. Once this truly sinks in, you will stop asking others to change in order for you to feel better. It's not their responsibility; it doesn't show how much they care; and no matter how hard they try, you might wind up feeling bad anyway.

We've already discussed a more basic point. As a leader, you must commit yourself to building relationships. That's a necessary starting point but one that many don't reach. The undermining belief here is that relationships are too hard. You can reverse this belief by realizing that relationships, hard or easy, amount to everything in life. If you convince yourself that you can be completely alone, you are deluded. Even if you escaped to a cabin at the North Pole surrounded by vast emptiness, you would carry all your past relationships with you in your memories, habits, personality, and expectations.

Every person is the sum total of relationships past and present. To take responsibility, a few guidelines apply:

> *Clearly see the difference between past and present.*
> *Don't inflict past relationships on present ones.*
> *Relate on the basis of shared positive values. Avoid*
> *   relating on the basis of prejudices and shared bias.*
> *As a leader, try to relate equally and impartially.*
> *Avoid making the other person wrong.*
> *Follow the Golden Rule: other people will sense when*
> *   you are treating them the way you would want to*
> *   be treated.*
> *Increase the other person's self-esteem.*

In a way, the last point has become a kind of psychological Golden Rule. We've covered how a leader fulfills specific needs in the hierarchy of need. But you will interact with others many times, and not every encounter is about need. What is common to every encounter is that one self makes contact with another self. Make sure that when you part, the other self feels nurtured, enhanced, validated, encouraged, or appreciated. This is the closest we come in everyday life to one soul touching another. Relationship is a vast subject, but this is its spiritual essence.

I AM RESPONSIBLE FOR MY ROLE IN SOCIETY.

So far your responsibilities have been intimate and personal, but when we consider society, many thousands of people are involved. Our connections become more invisible, too. You create an impact on society by casting a vote, choosing where to live, volunteering for certain causes, and giving to certain charities. But there has been a lot of recent research on connections that sociologists never anticipated. As a leader, you need to realize the power of "social contagion," a term invented by researchers to describe how influence spreads from one person to another.

At the level of common sense, we all know that gossip and rumor have lives of their own, as do urban legends. Yesterday's conspiracy theories give way to today's paranoid focus. But social contagion reaches deeper than common sense ever indicated. Moods, attitudes, and habits are involved. If you are around a depressed family member, for example, you are more likely than average to become depressed yourself. But that's also true if you know someone who has a depressed friend, even when the person you know isn't depressed.

This is a very strange finding, but the data support it. You run a higher risk of being overweight or taking up smoking if a friend of a friend is overweight or smokes cigarettes. No one can account for these third-hand and even fourth-hand influences. Yet these "degrees of separation" are actually degrees of bonding. Social contagion is real but invisible. It also cuts both ways. Positive influences have their own infectiousness, so if a friend of a friend has good lifestyle habits or an optimistic outlook, you are more likely to develop them, too. This means that if you want to be part of an invisible social network, it's good to choose the one with the most positive and far-reaching effects.

You are having an influence even when you don't sign up as an official participant.

Various catchphrases have cropped up to describe the power of influence. "Tipping point" and "critical mass" are among the most popular. They both refer to a kind of chain reaction. At a certain moment enough people believe something that its spread cannot be stopped. Innovators, politicians, advertisers, and movie studios are in the business of creating tipping points, but in any field the effect of critical mass is important. It takes a village to do anything, or rather it takes the social equivalent of cell division; ideas catch on by increasing exponentially. (It's no accident that popular videos on the Web "go viral," indicating their infectious spread.)

Social networking has become a necessity in the modern world, and the networks you join or create should reflect your level of awareness:

Join networks that specifically address your main purpose.

Make positive, detailed contributions.

Treat each message the way you would treat a personal encounter, with openness and respect.

Share your highest ideals and keep those ideals in mind every time you send a message. Each transmission should reflect your core values, or at least not run counter to them.

Resist the temptation to amplify destructive gossip, rumors, and paranoid theories.

Keep in close, regular touch with the members of the network that matter most to you. Don't take up more personal networking than you are able to deal with.

Although many types of messages are brief and fleeting, when you make extended contact, follow the golden rule of relationships: enhance the other person's self-esteem.

I AM RESPONSIBLE FOR MY IMMEDIATE ENVIRONMENT.

We project ourselves into our surroundings, so every situation has its own atmosphere. As soon as a new person enters a room, the atmosphere changes, if only a little. Leaders create big changes: their tone sets the kind of environment that others experience. It doesn't matter if you sit quietly and say nothing, your influence will still be powerful. But it can be difficult to read the effect you are having. After all, the only way that you've seen people interact all your life is with your being present. How they behave when you are subtracted from the equation is an unknown.

Spiritually, the projection that a person creates is total. You are the whole situation that you find yourself in, creator of a continual mirroring effect. You can choose to accept or reject this principle, but it's not very difficult to prove it to yourself. To do that, get into the habit of comparing "in here" and "out there." To be self-aware, you must ask questions that reconnect inside and outside. The two domains are never separate, but we keep them that way through lack of awareness. Let's take a look at four ways we shape our experience: mood, memory, expectation, and perception.

Mood: Is the situation connected to my mood? At one level we all see the world through glasses of different tints. The sunset doesn't look the same to someone who's depressed and someone who's in love. At a deeper level, the fact that you are outside looking at a sunset means that it is part of you; therefore, your mood not only colors the sunset, it creates it. That is, when you are depressed, you aren't looking at something beautiful and glorious without the ability to appreciate it: the sunset *is* depressing; for you, in this moment, it has no other way of being. Or think of someone you dearly love or heartily despise. When that person walks into the room, your feeling is part of her. As long as you are the observer, she takes on the quality of your mood.

Memory: Is the situation connected to something from my past? Your experience of the past creates the present. This, too, works at several levels. Obviously, when you see someone you recognize, you draw on memory; otherwise, the world would be full of strangers. It would also be full of strange objects. Indeed, it would be a strange world. Memory also tells you that a car isn't a painted lump of metal but a machine that you know how to drive. All recognition is memory. At a deeper level, you cannot undo memory: you can only see it for what it is. A book is something you know how to read. You can't make yourself turn the book back into a collection of meaningless marks on a page the way it was when you were two months old.

Expectation: Is the situation what I expected it to be? Except in rare instances, the answer is yes. Expectations precede involvement. As you get involved, your expectations guide what you think is happening. Imagine that you are about to meet a stranger. You hear that he is charming and witty. The moment before he walks into the room, however, someone whispers in our ear, "He's a well-known con man." The situation suddenly changes because your expectation has been altered. At a deeper level, your expectations actually shape what others are doing and saying. We subtly tune in to the expectations of others. We can sense whether they are going to be easy or difficult, open or self-involved, friendly or aloof. Silent signals shape all encounters. As for situations that defy expectation, usually the expectation was false or a projection: we are covering up fear, apprehension, suspicion, or doubts. The "surprise" fulfills these more real but hidden expectations; it should be no surprise that all at once you are aware of feelings you have denied and pushed out of sight.

Perception: Am I seeing the situation through tinted glasses? Here the rule is "Seeing it so makes it so." We're talking about the subtlest level of experience, because perception is creative. Our belief that we passively observe the world is mistaken. As neurologists are quick to point out, every quality in the world is created in the brain. Your visual cortex creates sunlight. By itself, the sun's radiation is a blank. It's just a band of frequencies in the electromagnetic field. With a different kind of brain, you might see the world lit up by magnetism, or temperature, or even gravity. Raw data must be translated into color, light, sound, texture, shapes, smells—indeed, everything you can possibly perceive.

Taken to its deepest spiritual conclusion, you are perceiving nothing but your creation. If that sounds unbelievable, reverse the proposition. Can you participate in anything you don't perceive? Neutrinos and gamma rays are passing through your body; hormone levels rise and fall; your metabolism regulates itself according to how warm the room is and what you ate for breakfast. You aren't participating in these events because you can't perceive them. The spiritual aspect of this is that your soul perceives everything; therefore it participates in everything. There is no difference between regulating your liver enzymes and regulating the events that will happen to you today and the people you'll meet. At the soul level, perception creates everything. You may protest that you cannot possibly be the creator of a rock and its hardness or a stranger on the bus and the words he will speak. Yet you control both in your dreams.

Dreams are a domain of perception. They can have sight, sound, touch, taste, and smell. But those sensations aren't separate from us; we are the source of our dreams and all that happens inside them. In the world's wisdom traditions, the same is true of reality "out there." The same brain that creates every detail of the dream environment is responsible for every detail of the waking environment. If you don't feel ready to make this spiritual leap, there's no need to do so. Just keep testing whether or not the situation is you. The deeper you go, the more you will be convinced that it is.

I AM RESPONSIBLE FOR MY SPEECH.

The words you utter are events in their own right. They have an effect on other people, which should never be forgotten. The reason I've saved this responsibility for next to last is that your words unfold thought, emotion, perception, relationships, and social role. Everything that came before is involved. Linguists tell us that speech does not serve only to communicate ideas. A simple phrase is multi-dimensional. Think of everything we discover through tone of voice, for example. In a moment you can assess fairly accurately whether the speaker is happy or sad, engaged or aloof, warm or cold, friend or stranger, open or closed, available or unavailable—and that barely scratches the surface. (One prominent psychiatrist who had a long-running radio program claimed that he could diagnose callers' personality problems simply by hearing them give their names.)

When you take responsibility for your speech, you are going beyond just its content. This can be difficult. We all resist such comments as "I don't like your tone," "What are you trying to say?" "I know what this is really about," and "You're saying one thing and meaning another." What bothers us is the reminder that we are revealing more than we want to, and yet we all know that this is going on. It's natural for speech to be revealing on the level of how we feel, what we want, what we'd like to hide, and what we expect the other person to understand. A leader takes responsibility for these additional dimensions.

Once you take on this responsibility, two options are open to you. You can discipline and control your speech, letting others receive only what you want them to. Or you can accept that being open is better, in which case you let people read into you what they want to read into you. The second option makes you more vulnerable, but it's the best choice, because people are going to read into you all kinds of things that are beyond your control. The impression that anybody has of you is his own creation. Since this is inescapable, shine your light as fully as you can. Keep as little as possible in the shadows. Don't create ambivalent or inscrutable feelings on purpose. Be consistent in how you speak. Observe the amenities of courtesy and respect for others. These are the necessaries of owning your words and the effect they have on others. Speech is a window on the soul. You will succeed far more by opening the window than by keeping it shut.

I AM RESPONSIBLE FOR MY BODY.

You might think that taking care of your body is so basic that it should come first on the list. I've placed it last for a reason. Your body isn't a machine made of flesh and blood. Seen from the soul level, it is the projection of your consciousness. In fact, it is the most complete projection of who you are, more so than your thoughts, feelings, and words, which come and go. Your body is a constant projection of you in the world. Every cell eavesdrops on your thoughts. You cannot respond to the world without affecting your tissues and organs. Without a body you cannot connect to the universe; therefore your body is the vehicle of your evolution.

Every leader wants to be tuned in. You can't tune in without a body—that much is self-evident—but the quality of how you tune in is quite subtle. The loss of an hour's sleep, for example, distorts reflexes and blurs perception almost as much as losing half a night's sleep. A heavy, fatty meal with a glass of wine dulls the mind and makes decisions less reliable. Depleted biological energy, whether from disease, fatigue, or stress, can't help but deplete mental energy. The mind-body connection isn't like a lamp plugged into a wall socket. It's a hundred billion neurons all plugged into one another and then into trillions of cells throughout the body. The same is true of our interactions with the world. All feedback loops begin and end with the body.

Once you see your body as a projection of all that you are, taking responsibility for it is no longer the choice to sign up for the gym or ordering fish instead of steak. Think of your body as metabolizing the world, taking in more than just food, water, and air; your body is metabolizing every experience. This is because every experience uses energy supplied by food, air, and water. Chemical reactions transform raw data into "my" experience; you take possession by literally internalizing every sight and sound. What was once "out there" is now "in here," and thanks to cellular memory, it is likely to remain with you for a long time.

This perspective doesn't change the basics of a healthy lifestyle, which are familiar: a balanced diet low in fat, regular exercise with a focus on cardiovascular impact, good sleep, meditation, and stress management. However, it brings you closer to a simple truth: your body exists to serve you. But it can only give what it has to give, no more. If you see your body as consciousness that has taken material form, it's clear that it has much more to give you through its awareness. The physical gift of awareness is present when the body is light, bright, flexible, energized, balanced, and quick to respond. Since these are all qualities you want as a leader, one way to have them is by taking responsibility for your body.

We've covered eight areas of life that you are responsible for, but please note that they don't add to your burden as a leader. Each can be mastered effortlessly once you are committed to being guided by your soul. As you evolve, divisions disappear. Mind, body, behavior, and speech begin to flow together. Then you begin to master not just the art of leadership but the art of living. Your soul starts to influence you in everything you do, and as it does, the gap between you and your soul closes. Wholeness starts to dominate. In the next section we'll see how life is transformed in wholeness. The miraculous becomes normal; the field of possibilities loses every limitation. Before that can happen, however, you must be responsible for all that you are and want to be.

THE LESSONS OF RESPONSIBILITY

• Leading from the soul means taking responsibility for your evolution and the evolution of others. Evolution is an unstoppable force. By aligning with it, you will benefit yourself and everyone around you.

• In every area of life, from mind and body to personal relationships and the social role that you play, your soul can bring continual progress. No aspect of the situation is ever left out.

• In spiritual terms, the situation is you. Every experience reflects your level of consciousness. The inner and outer world merge at the level of the soul. Being responsible ultimately comes down to accepting the wholeness of life.

WHAT TO DO TODAY

This chapter outlines a plan for encouraging your own evolution and the evolution of others. But this involves the reverse as well—not discouraging the force of evolution. You are the soul of the group. Your behavior acts like a magnet, attracting similar behavior. In spiritual terms the impulse to grow and expand is an unstoppable force, yet we can resist it and make choices that undermine our growth. When a leader stands against evolution, the whole group will be affected.

Today take some time to look closely at yourself and ask if you are displaying any of the following behaviors that serve to undermine evolution.

10 Discouraging Behaviors

I obsess over risks. I keep worrying about what can go wrong.

I don't face a problem, even when it is staring me in the face.

I secretly want the group to do what I want.

I haven't taken responsibility for my last bad decision and its consequences.

I blame people around me; I make excuses for myself.

I crave approval and reassurance.

I don't delegate authority, or I delegate it but keep a tight grip on all decisions.

I look out for myself more than for the group.

I only listen to the same few voices in my inner circle.

I find myself lying or covering up the truth.

You must be vigilant about these traps because in mild or severe form, they lower the group's consciousness. Physics uses the term *entropy* to describe how energy dissipates in the universe. Wrong behavior has its own quiet way of sapping energy. But eventually there will be a price to pay, as the group falters and stagnates, or becomes unfocused and divisive.

If you adopt evolutionary behavior instead, you will be serving the soul's purpose, which is to raise the consciousness of the group.

Your soul gave you a desire to live a greater truth. In practical terms, you need to reverse each discouraging behavior, as follows:

10 EVOLUTIONARY BEHAVIORS

Don't obsess over risks. Keep your focus on positive outcomes.

Face problems when they are still in seed form.

Be attuned to the group's needs first and foremost.

Take responsibility for your last bad decision, and then let it go.

Don't blame others or make excuses for yourself.

Be immune to the good or bad opinion of others.

Show confidence in those to whom you delegate authority.

Be generous in giving rather than taking.

Open yourself to every avenue of information and wise counsel.

Promise yourself to tell the truth, particularly when it's most tempting to lie.

Evolutionary behavior can't be forced—it has to be cultivated. Many successful leaders learn how to evolve naturally, as the result of being tuned in to their inner voices and guided by intuition. Destructive behavior has a way of weeding out bad leaders through failure. But the behaviors listed above are aligned with the evolutionary power of the soul, invisibly bringing that power to aid and support you. Right behavior keeps you subtly aligned with evolution itself, the tendency for all things to organically grow and expand.

Seven

S = SYNCHRONICITY

Every leader needs support, and no support is more power-ful than that provided by the soul. It offers a continuous stream of small and large gifts from the mystery. This is the work of synchronicity, the unseen intelligence that puts you in the right place at the right time. The first six letters of L-E-A-D-E-R-S gave you the preparedness for a leap in awareness, the leap that allows you to live from the level of your soul. Here miracles are normal. Invisible powers come to your aid. They make your vision a certainty.

Successful visionaries expect miracles because they trust in constant support from the soul. It is a natural and easy way to live. You allow your true self to unfold; then you can open the same path to those you lead and serve.

As we will see, synchronicity is never accidental; it has a purpose. It validates that your motive is true. It proves that your trust in the soul is well placed. As your aware-ness expands, you will receive messages from the soul that are unmistakable. All you need to do is to open yourself up and receive them.

This final aspect of leadership is more mysterious than the others. Successful leaders can all look back at small miracles in their lives, but successful visionaries look back at major miracles. A small miracle involves a stroke of luck, or being in the right place at the right time. A major miracle is very different. The impossible turns into a certainty, and higher guidance intervenes and alters the course of your life. The soul can create miracles for anyone; the limitations are in ourselves. Remove those limitations, and nothing will ever be the same again.

Leading from the soul involves having the kind of support that is hidden from most people. This doesn't mean trying to get God on your side. God is on everyone's side, because God is how we conceive of the infinite power that organizes creation. If the soul is your link to this power, it can arrange any event in time and space. The term for such arranged events is *synchronicity*. The basic definition, "a meaningful coincidence," really isn't adequate to describe what happens. Coincidences link two unlikely happenings—for example, two strangers meet and have the same last name, or went to the same schools. Synchronicity, on the other hand, alters events to bring in more meaning. Two people meet, and one has the answer to a problem the other hasn't been able to solve, and in the process a tiny seed of an idea is given an enormous opportunity to grow. A personal dream is suddenly given the chance to become reality.

When leaders are asked why they are outstanding successes, they reply using *good luck* more often than any other phrase—they realize that they have led exceptional lives but have no model to explain it. Synchronicity is the right model. It describes a fundamental process in the universe. Your body depends upon unimaginable synchronicity. Out of one hundred billion brain cells, each looks out for its own food, air, and water, as a paramecium or amoeba looks out for itself in a green pond on a mild summer day. Yet somehow brain cells act in perfect coordination. Every thought is an exquisitely choreographed dance.

Billions of neurons are coordinating in order for you to read this sentence. No visible system connects them. Synchronicity has created a major miracle on an almost invisible scale. If it were to occur on a large scale, it would be as if every person on earth said the same sentence at the same moment without planning it in advance. Coincidence cannot come close to describing what is happening here.

At truly synchronous moments, the universe is embracing you, and you see who you really are. The real you is not separate and isolated. The world you experience is not random but one where events are constantly being shuffled to bring you the best result possible. Leaders are expected to produce results, so it's not surprising that the greatest leaders share the secret of synchronicity. They rely on invisible powers to come to their aid. Your personal vision needs the same support, and you can learn to cultivate it. Miracles in your life indicate that you have a strong connection to your soul. Regard them as sudden leaps in your evolution. Once you expect synchronicity to be there when it is needed, it will be. Then you can pass the benefit on to everyone around you.

UPGRADING THE NORMAL

To maximize your access to the miraculous, you can take practical steps. If you follow them, you can become a successful visionary, the goal that gives this book its reason for being.

THE PATH TO MIRACLES

Regard synchronicity as normal.
Look for the hidden message.
Go where you are guided.
Be here in the present.
Understand the harmony of contained conflicts.
Encourage unity; discourage divisions.
Align yourself with a new belief: "I am the world."

As you can see, some of these steps are internal; they involve changing your old beliefs and expectations. Others are external; they involve how you act in the world and relate to others.

Regard synchronicity as normal.

Your first step is to reverse any belief that synchronicity is abnormal. Without it life couldn't exist. Ecology is exquisitely coordinated. A cat put inside a sealed jar will die from lack of oxygen. A fern put into a sealed jar will die from lack of carbon dioxide. But put them together, and they will survive. On a planetary scale, this delicate interdependence goes far beyond mere survival: Nature provides a setting for all species to thrive and evolve. You are part of the same stream of life. You were designed to thrive and evolve in the ecology that surrounds and enmeshes you. Many would say that the events of a lifetime are random. Certainly in the materialist worldview randomness dominates: intelligence is a secondary accident that somehow produced the human brain through trial and error. If you accept this worldview, of course you would regard synchronicity as no more than a small example of an intriguing coincidence.

Despite accidents and chance, however, in our everyday experience, we rely on awareness, wherever it comes from. Theory is one thing; practice is another. Our lives mean something. We don't have to claim that a higher power is at work; it's much simpler to say that intelligence exists everywhere. Think about a synchronous event in your life, when you met a stranger who turned out to play a very significant role. If pure chance were at work, the odds would be millions to one. It is simpler—and according to the principle of Occam's razor therefore more logical—to say that the meeting was meant to be, that a guiding intelligence is working invisibly, shaping the event to serve a purpose. In the world's wisdom traditions, this explanation extends to a person's whole life. Successful visionaries adopt this belief because it has proved valid in their own lives.

Visionaries feel connected to a larger purpose.
They experience a dream coming true.
They have prayed and received an answer.
They sense that their lives are deeply meaningful.
They feel guided from within.
They rely upon significant synchronicity.
They walk the path that was destined for them.

You don't have to convince yourself that these things are true. They become true, easily and naturally, as consciousness expands. In fact they become commonplace. Synchronicity isn't a form of divine favoritism that puts a few privileged people ahead of the rest of us. Everyone is totally and equally supported from the level of the soul.

Look for the hidden message.

If your soul is sending you messages at this moment, you need to receive them. This is no different from having a conversation with someone. If you ignore what the other person says, the dialogue comes to an end. In most lives, dialogue with the soul is very tenuous and shaky. Being able to receive the soul's messages makes a real difference, but the difference is easier to describe by what is absent than by what is present.

You don't feel uncared for and unloved.
You aren't isolated and alone.
Your actions aren't dictated by habit and random
impulses.

Your existence has stopped being a riddle.
You are not a victim.

I could have used the positive form of each statement
("You feel cared for and loved," "Your existence becomes
meaningful," etc.), but I want to emphasize the problems
that have gone away. There are moments when changes are
so easy to see, they can't be missed. The first day you re-
cover from a cold, you can't help but notice that you aren't
stuffed up and achy anymore. But over time this contrast
disappears. The same is true spiritually. You may suddenly
notice that you no longer feel lonely or misunderstood or
unsafe in the world, if those were once problems for you.
But most of the time there is simply a flow of connections
that feels unremarkable.

"Look for the hidden message" means taking a moment
to notice the negative things that have slipped away: fear,
uncertainty, threat, anger, resentment, envy, struggle, external obstacles, inner voices that criticize and judge you,
traumatic memories, toxic relationships, guilt, and shame.
It's a long list, and most of us rarely dwell on it. As your
awareness expands, however, you will notice that items on
the list will steadily fade away, and your life will be more
smoothly and easily knit together. That is a sign that you
are in true dialogue with the soul.

Go where you are guided.

Once the dialogue with your soul is set up, it leads somewhere. It guides you on your path. But if your guide is

silent, how do you know if you are heeding it? The clearest indication is that your ego no longer dominates your thinking. We've discussed the ego in Chapter Five; contrasting its focus on "I, me, and mine" with transpersonal values, where the perspective is "us." As awareness expands, your ego's role becomes more and more that of the observer. Less and less will it make demands that you must heed.

The soul's guidance doesn't come in the form of instructions, such as "Don't be so selfish" or "Think about other people more." Being silent, the soul works differently—it makes old habits less satisfying. The sensation is like walking on solid ground that suddenly stops supporting you. Someone might make you angry, for example, but instead of going off on them and feeling justified in your anger, you find that the feeling of anger just evaporates. Guidance is the gradual melting away of ego and all its familiar responses: anger, fear, resentment, jealousy, and the constant need to compare yourself to others.

You can see yourself being guided in the following stages:

The Stages of Personal Change

1. *Being stuck*: I am used to acting this way. It fits who I am. The situation calls for me to react this way. What's the problem? *I* don't have one.

2. *First doubts*: My reaction doesn't feel quite right. I have twinges of guilt. It's as if I can't help myself, but I wish I could.

3. *Self-questioning*: I need to stop reacting this way. It's pointless; it no longer feels right. If I am ever going to change, these old habits have to go.

4. *Seeking change*: I catch myself reacting and do my best to stop. Others know I want to change, and they help and encourage me. I notice people who don't react the way I do. I want to be like them.

5. *Finding change*: I have more control over my reactions. I have learned how to let go. I get no satisfaction from the way I used to behave. I don't even recognize the person I used to be.

6. *Reintegration*: I'm new. There are traces of my old reactions, but they barely influence me. I don't think about who I used to be. I am clear about who I am and happy with the person I see inside.

Although synchronicity is experienced privately and subjectively, being familiar with these six stages of personal change is very useful to any leader. As a leader, your role is to motivate change, so you need to recognize its symptoms. People rarely have a sudden epiphany that causes them, Scrooge-like, to exchange the very bad for the very good. In real life, Scrooge flirts with being nicer and less stingy, takes small steps in a new direction, and often backslides. But change is occurring. As a leader, you can encourage it every step of the way by noticing and being sympathetic. Look upon yourself as midwife to a fragile birth. Express your appreciation at the smallest signs of the new as it emerges.

Be here in the present.

In recent years the power of now has become a favorite spiritual topic. Being present has an undeniable appeal. Joy and happiness can only occur right this moment. If you dwell on past joys and wish for future happiness, they are not yours now. But the present is tricky. By definition, *now* lasts only a split second before it turns into the past.

There are instances when people experience being totally present. Their existence becomes free of all burdens. An inner illumination fills everything they see. The mundane is transformed into the extraordinary, the dull into the brilliant. At the same time, however, they feel a disturbing loss of balance. The present moment can feel a lot like freefall. There's no rope to hang on to connecting past, present, and future. Nothing is certain anymore.

Therefore it's better to adapt to the present by stages. Your soul is always in the present, so it's not the now that you must seize. It cannot be seized anyway. Respect the part of you that wants to cling to the familiar. Encourage the part that wants to be open to the new. Here's another way to enter into the process:

• Be centered. If you notice that you have lost your center, pause and return there.

• Remain open to your surroundings—let information and impressions flow in freely.

• If you find yourself saying or doing what you habitually do, catch yourself. Pause and stand back. It's okay not to react. Leave an open space for something new.

• Appreciate the present moment. Notice what is nourishing about it. Take a moment to really look at the people you are with.

• If judgment, anger, or anxiety starts to color your mood, don't resist. Tell the negative feeling that you will pay attention to it later. Follow up your promise by contacting the feeling again to see if it still needs to be dealt with.

• Expect the best. Look for positive signals in the situation. These signals may come from other people, but they can also be simply a good feeling in the air. Ask that good feeling to come in and uplift you.

• Don't open doors to the past. Nostalgia and reliving old times can be pleasant, but the bad parts about the past are given entry at the same time. If old memories come to you, look at them and let them be what they are, but don't do anything active with them.

By meditating and remaining centered, you will get glimpses of the present quite soon. The more you expand your awareness, the more naturally you will be present without effort. One of the most obvious signs is that you feel lighter physically, but any experience of being carefree, safe, welcomed, filled with light, uplifted, or inspired is a gift from the present moment. In time these moments will merge into a continual experience. When that happens, the now will be your home forever.

Understand the harmony of contained conflicts.

The soul doesn't engage in conflict. When you feel pulled to defend your notion of right and wrong, you can certainly keep it and achieve some beneficial things. There are many wrongs to confront in this world. But you won't be acting from the soul. Spiritually, the way to deal with the eternal war between light and dark, right and wrong, creation and destruction is to go beyond the battle.

When this happens, you see that explicit enemies are implicit allies: neither side can exist without the other. There is no good to fight for unless someone else is made to be bad or wrong. I know that this is a difficult shift; we can all think of horrors that seem absolute and must be defeated. But let go of moral arguments for a moment, and regard how Nature works. When two animals are predator and prey, like the lion and the gazelle, life encloses them in the same circle. When a rose blooms, it is paired with molds that turn the dead blossoms into compost. Mold isn't beautiful; decomposition stinks, unlike the fragrance of a rose. Yet without the other, neither can exist. To go beyond good and evil is simply to see the larger whole that embraces opposites. Wholeness contains conflicts, but they serve the greater good by keeping creation and destruction in balance.

One reason we can miss the opportunities that the soul provides is that we shut out experience in advance, labeling certain things as unacceptable. For peaceful people it is unacceptable to use force. For self-contained people it is unacceptable to lose control of one's emotions. If you look at your own value system, you can make a personal list of "what I will never do." Take a moment and make such a list. Once you've finished, realize this: you are tied to the things you resist. The tie is unconscious but still powerful. What if you had an abusive parent and grew up swearing to yourself that you would never inflict the kind of harm you suffered through? Yes, you would consciously become a better person, but unconsciously you would have defined yourself through your abuser, limiting your freedom to experience everything.

Resist a moral interpretation. I'm not saying that you should choose to abuse others, not at all. Rather, look at the closed compartments that need to be open. For example, many children of abuse find it very hard to trust anyone after they grow up; trust is a closed compartment. Others find it hard to show compassion for "bad" people; still others adopt rigid codes of behavior that they impose on themselves and others. When the soul brings messages of compassion, openness, and nonjudgment, the person shuts them out because they don't fit her fixed beliefs. There is resistance instead of receptivity.

This is understandable, but in terms of synchronicity, compartmentalizing your mind is very limiting. Now you receive only what is acceptable. And if you already know what is good and bad in advance, you have no real need for a soul. You have no intention of growing beyond your fixed belief system. But the soul is all about growing. To be receptive to the harmony of contained conflicts, practice the following steps:

• Take the long view. Try to see how the worst things in your past benefited you. Have faith that setbacks in the present will also benefit you down the road.

• Realize that everyone is defined by his level of consciousness. What looks easy to change from your perspective looks binding from his.

• Accept that everyone is doing the best she can from her level of awareness. This can be difficult when others are doing things you strongly disapprove of. But you can come closer to acceptance if you add a second point: no matter how badly people are behaving, they, too, have souls, which means that at some level they yearn for positive change.

• Investigate in depth how Nature balances creation and destruction. Gestation, birth, growth, maturity, and decay exist at every level of the cosmos. Instead of attaching yourself only to one aspect of this cycle, resolve to embrace it all. This is how your soul views reality.

• On a behavioral level, fight the good fight if it calls out to you, but resist becoming a polarizing force. Whatever it takes, see some good in your adversary. Show respect, and bend over backward to negotiate before the fight begins. Avoid relationships with people who can see good only in their position. Anyone who vilifies the other side is creating enemies, which is ultimately more destructive than anything else. You may be victorious, but your enemies will persist after the conflict is over.

Encourage unity; discourage divisions.

In the section on team building, we discussed the value of negotiating differences so that the group doesn't splinter. Now we have to look deeper. You have taken on the part of leading from the soul because you are on a personal journey, the journey to higher consciousness. As seen by the soul, your vision will ultimately be fulfilled only when you reach enlightenment. Enlightenment is about the reconciliation of opposites. Unity replaces differences; wholeness becomes a living reality. At that point everything human will be part of you.

Knowing that this is the end point of your journey, act as if you have already arrived. Be a force for bringing opposites together. Opposites begin with you yourself. They find voice in some typical responses:

> *I have an angel on one shoulder and a devil on the other.*
>
> *I feel ambivalent. I can't commit.*
>
> *Some days I love the person I'm with. Other days there's no love at all.*
>
> *I swing between self-esteem and feeling unworthy.*
>
> *Am I real or a fraud? I'm afraid that somebody is going to see through me one day and expose me.*
>
> *I'm grown up, but I still feel as helpless as a child.*
>
> *If others love me, why do I feel so lonely?*

These are the beliefs of someone who is divided against himself. Self-division gets projected outward. It's impossible to truly accept others when you have serious doubts about yourself. This is one of the few hard-and-fast rules about spirituality. Behind it lies a larger truth: you can give only what you have to give. If you don't have self-esteem, you can't find worth in others. The same is true for love, compassion, and forgiveness. All will be yours to give once you apply them to yourself.

Society doesn't teach us how to grow spiritually, and therefore most people get stuck in the endless games that opposites play. Most leaders, in fact, are trapped in divisiveness because it serves them. They foster winners instead of losers. They want more for "us" and less for "them." They identify rivals to beat, market shares to grab, weak companies to gobble up, and areas where no concession is possible.

Here, leading from the soul is simple: if you have to tear somebody down in order to feel bigger, don't do it. Seek positive reasons to build up your situation without needing an adversary. Heal your own divisions, and you will radiate a sense of worth that has no need to tear down anyone else. The soul's motto is "I am enough," and as your awareness expands, you will become enough. From that point on, you will exhibit the generosity and compassion for the fallen that is a hallmark of the greatest visionaries.

Align yourself with a new belief: "I am the world."

Here too you can live the goal before you reach it. None of us were raised to believe that we were the world. The statement sounds almost unintelligible. Even the ego would blush at such a gross exaggeration. But saying "I am the world" is actually humble. It's your acknowledgment that you are a thread in the tapestry of life. Just as the complete code of DNA is enclosed in every cell, you contain every aspect of consciousness. What the world is made of, so it is with you. You leave nothing out except by choice. There are many such choices, however, and we've all made them.

Every label you identify with excludes something else: my race, my gender, my nationality, my education, my status. Each label is one thing, but in possessing that one thing, you push away many other things: all other races, nationalities, education levels, social roles, and people of the opposite gender. Labels are defensive. It's no accident that they allow you to reject everything that is "not me." Life feels much safer when you draw a circle around your identity and don't step outside it.

There are two types of leaders, then: those who defend the circle and those who look beyond it. The first stance is much easier to adopt; people are usually insecure without defenses, so the tighter their circle is, the better they feel. The second role belongs to the visionary. It speaks to a deeper yearning. Inside, we all know that human beings are one. The same joy and suffering infuse every life. This knowledge is something we try to shut out, but we cannot fully turn it away because being human comes from the soul. To insist that the outside world is "not me" is unreal. No matter how tightly you draw your family, tribe, race, or nationality around you, the result is not greater safety but isolation and illusion.

Real freedom lies outside the circle. It's the people you never expected to bond with, the viewpoints that are completely different from your own, and the ideas you never considered that will liberate you. We speak of meeting needs, both yours and the group's. But needs are only stepping-stones to one goal: liberating the spirit within. "I am the world" affirms that your real nature is spirit. It speaks of wanting to experience everything. If you align yourself with this deep yearning, you will be guided by the soul every day of your life. Nothing can stand in your way when you drop the foolish notion that you must accept boundaries. By nature you are unbounded.

At journey's end you will be whole. All the inner divisions that gave rise to doubt and conflict will be healed. So what good does it do to postpone that day? The unknown is a magnet drawing you closer to liberation. When you look for the next horizon, you are reaching for a new place inside yourself. Each new place whispers that the soul is near, until one day you merge with it, and then your being and the eternal Being are one.

THE LESSONS OF SYNCHRONICITY

- Leading from the soul means gaining the support of invisible powers. You expect miracles to come to your aid. You trust in your soul to organize events to bring about the best results.

- Synchronicity isn't mystical. It is evidence of the hidden intelligence that pervades the universe. This intelligence coordinates everything in creation, and if you are open to it, it can coordinate the creation of your vision.

- In spiritual terms, every visionary is on a personal journey. Each need that you fulfill, for yourself or for the group, is a stepping-stone to liberation. When you are free, you will be whole. Looking back, you will see that every miracle, large or small, was the exact thing you needed to reach fulfillment.

WHAT TO DO TODAY

Synchronicity is normal once you remove the obstacles that block it. Today you can do that by divesting yourself of labels. When you say "I am X," you are labeling yourself. The more strongly you identify with any label, the more closed off you will be. You will miss all kinds of experiences that fall into the category of "not me," which in reality are just not your label, which is a very different thing. In the absence of labels, you will be much more comfortable with everyone and everything. "All of this is me" is the ideal way to live. To divest yourself of labels, here are some suggestions:

• Instead of being labeled by your name, give anonymously to a good cause.

• Instead of being labeled by your race, volunteer for a cause that helps minority members.

• Instead of being labeled by gender, join a group that aids battered women or provides shelter for homeless men.

• Instead of being labeled by your job, spend some time doing a job that is much lower on the prestige scale.

• Instead of being labeled by your money, go to the poorest part of town and volunteer there.

Many of these suggestions qualify as good works, but primarily they are intended to take you beyond a narrow sense of who you are. If you carry your labels with you, no matter where you go you will be constrained by them. So approach these suggestions with the intent of becoming part of the scene, engaging at the level of shared spirit. Measure your success by ridding yourself of labels, which also divests others of theirs. Does that seem to be happening?

A leader should aspire to be the soul of the group. You can attain this goal in any group once you see the soul in everyone else. In the phrase "all men are created equal," the verb is in the present tense. It's not that all men (and women) "*were* created equal." Creation happens at every moment. Life refreshes and renews us. If you allow this process to touch you deeply, you won't need labels of any kind. To be a wave on the ocean of life will be glorious enough.

PART TWO

TWO
WHO LEAD FROM
THE SOUL

Eight

JEREMY MOON,
Founder and CEO of Icebreaker

Icebreaker is the little company that put New Zealand's merino wool on the map. Nothing about the budding enterprise was conventional. When Icebreaker was ten years old, in 2005, a local reporter described its headquarters in Wellington, on New Zealand's South Island, as having "the look and feel of a gigantic student party," while founder Jeremy Moon was "wide-eyed and tousle-haired." Yet behind this youth-oriented casualness, he was doing some serious rethinking about how a company should be in the world, and what modern enterprise should stand for.

Jeremy grew his company by making every step part of his own journey, in which a vision unfolded first in consciousness and then took shape in the real world of business. His is the story of a young man who had a single experience that changed his life. Today Icebreaker is a massive team effort, focused on building the most sustainable clothing business in the world. It uses beautiful, renewable, biodegradable merino wool sourced from the Southern Alps of New Zealand. As Jeremy sees it, this effort is wholly true to that first experience that ignited his enthusiasm.

WHEN I STARTED Icebreaker, I was twenty-four, broke, and had absolutely no idea what I was doing. But I was driven by a passion for what I saw was possible, and a belief that I could make it happen. That passion was ignited by a meeting with a merino sheep farmer. Across the dining table, he threw me a T-shirt made from a merino wool fabric he'd designed himself. It felt soft and sensuous and nothing like regular wool. The shirt could be washed in the washing machine rather than by hand; it was silky and soft rather than itchy, and it felt light instead of heavy.

I thought, "Wow! This is an amazingly beautiful, practical, natural material. This is a product I could sell around the world." You see, from the first moment, I imagined myself flying around the globe and having a great time. I had no idea how a business based on merino wool could work, but I had a strong feeling that I could make it happen. My training is in cultural anthropology and marketing, so I was interested in the meaning of objects, and I knew how to develop plans for bringing ideas alive.

I buried myself for two months in my bedroom, setting out how I could build an international brand from New Zealand. This took vision. New Zealand isn't a great place to build a company from—no one knows where we are, and we don't have any neighbors. But it's a great place to live and connect with the world. My business plan set out the basic steps that would have to happen to turn this dream into a reality. Who would be on the team? How would we raise money? How could we set up manufacturing and sell our products?

I screwed up the courage to quit my job and borrow seed money. The going was slow. It took five years to get a sense of what I was doing. Those years were pure desire and perseverance. I put in huge amounts of hard work and faced equally huge amounts of frustration and angst. I worked seventy to one hundred hours a week. I had to commit myself totally to the business because if it failed, I would have been bankrupt. Never once did I lose my ability to see the big picture. I never doubted that it was possible to succeed. My mantra was "This will work if I don't screw it up." I took full responsibility for my future.

I've learned a few things about leadership over the past fifteen years, and I'd like to share them with you. For me, leadership has been an evolving journey. Someone once told me that when you're running your own business, you have more breakthroughs and breakdowns in a month than most people have in a year. It certainly felt like that to me. Every few years I've had to critically review my own performance and that of the business to find better ways to lead the people I work with, and to provide better products for our customers.

I didn't start off wanting to be a leader. Rather, I connected with merino wool fiber on a deep level because of my identity as a New Zealander, my love of adventure, and my belief in nature. Leadership began when I had to enroll others in the Icebreaker concept. Money wasn't everything. I wanted people who cared and could help me. I had the ideas and the belief, but I didn't have the experience or the wisdom. Friends introduced me to their fathers who had been successful in business. One of them, a banker, asked me where my financials were. "What are financials?" I said. He offered to show me, and after three weeks of coaching, we had our first financial projections.

An early investor taught me how important employees were in business. I discovered it was critical to make everyone feel a part of Icebreaker, and I learned to run it as an extended family business. This appealed to me because I come from a strong family, and I wanted something that people could share in.

I put more than half of my initial capital into design. People thought I was mad, but more than anything else I wanted to create a deep, guiding brand story that was true and real. It was the story of a fiber grown on an animal that lived in the mountains of New Zealand, a fiber that could be developed into a clothing system that enabled people to go back into the mountains and reconnect with nature. We mined this deep and powerful cycle to create a compelling visual story that inspired the creation of the product. I loved it. I felt alive. My creativity was awakening.

For a country known for three things—adventure, natural beauty, and sheep—it's ironic that the entire outdoor clothing market in New Zealand was dominated by synthetics based on polyester and polypropylene. Why couldn't we wear something natural? Merino was a high-performance technical fiber that no one knew about. This was a great possibility, but the barriers to entry were huge. When I stepped into the marketplace, synthetics were king and wool was dead. It was up to me to convince people otherwise.

My first employee was Michelle Mitchell, a good friend who had such confidence in what I was doing that she gave up her law career to join me. Together we began to develop the core values of the business. Michelle told me, "A person with integrity is the same person at work as they are at play." I found this idea inspiring and immediately committed myself to putting it at the heart of Icebreaker. We opened ourselves to information from all sides. Our retailers taught us about the garment industry and gave me feedback on what worked and what didn't. Our suppliers taught us how to make clothes, how to use a warehouse, and how to deliver our goods. I was also learning from the other people who were joining the business. Some nights I was so excited I couldn't sleep. I felt my mind and soul expanding.

We chewed through most of our capital the first year and had forty retail customers by the second year, when the first revenue started coming in. In our third year three more employees were added, all young and inexperienced. Nothing seemed to work out the way we wanted it to, and everything was difficult. There were frustrations and tears, and lots and lots of late nights. But we were determined that Icebreaker would succeed. Slowly we learned how to work together as a team. We started experimenting with styling. We'd put garments on the table and arrange chopped-up bits of fabric on top to see what they looked like. Not surprisingly, our initial styling was very simple, but there was a certain beauty in that: it was honest, it was functional, and the fabric looked and felt beautiful.

We knew we were onto something special because our customers kept coming back for more. They told us their Icebreaker garments felt fantastic, worked brilliantly, lasted for ages, and were the best things they'd ever worn. A major change came when we started adding color to our products. I know, it's unbelievable that a clothing company didn't realize that color was important. Our first garments were blue and white, and then we added green, red, and black. ("Who's going to buy black?" I said. Now it's our best-selling color.)

As we grew, we discovered that when lightweight merino garments are worn together, air is trapped in between each layer, increasing the level of insulation— the layers lock together like a single garment, only warmer. It was a breakthrough, and it inspired us to evolve Icebreaker from an underwear range to a full layering system. Fifteen years on we now have offices in eight countries, we buy one quarter of the fine merino wool produced in New Zealand, we export our clothing to thirty countries, and we have millions of customers around the world. I've pledged that over the next fifteen years we will achieve extraordinary things and help reshape the face of business in the process.

For me, leadership started off as passion for an idea. Now it's about inspiring others to unlock their potential. I'm proud to say that the key people who built Icebreaker with me in those early days are still critical parts of the business. Another 250 employees have joined them. It's this team, along with our suppliers, customers, and our core values, that will determine what Icebreaker will become in the future.

JEREMY MOON AND L-E-A-D-E-R-S

After recounting his journey with Icebreaker, Jeremy analyzed his experience of being a leader using the acronym L-E-A-D-E-R-S. His response was detailed and inspiring at the same time.

Look and listen: At the outset I asked myself two essential questions: whom should we listen to, and why? The product didn't exist yet, so I had to listen to what was happening around me. Icebreaker's customers wanted a product that was real and authentic. They told us they wanted clothing that was high performance and built to last, that would help them reconnect to nature.

I discovered our customers liked sharing their

knowledge with a young person who was hungry to learn. My first customer told me that I was a good listener. Being a good listener was a win/win situation, and a great way to build a relationship.

I also listened to Icebreaker's board of directors, which meets for half a day once a month. They asked the big questions: What will Icebreaker look like in three years' time? Are we investing enough in the future? What is the internal health of the organization? What strategic issues need to be addressed? When I was deep in the trenches of the day-to-day detail of running a business, those questions made me focus on the bigger picture. For me, leadership has always been about asking the right questions to trigger the next evolution.

The volume of questions slowed down as the picture became clearer and I developed my ability to lead others, but it's still crucial to ask sharper, deeper questions. What is really important? How can a business contribute to society? How can an organization be a vehicle of consciousness? The evolving journey never ends; therefore you can never stop looking and listening.

Emotional Bonding: The world has gotten faster, and there are many more technologies, but business hasn't really changed that much. It's all about relationships. Icebreaker's relationships are with suppliers, retailers, and customers. We don't advertise, and yet we've managed to build a good-sized business based just on positive word of mouth.

We depend upon building an emotional bond. One way was by setting up Baacode, a program that lets customers trace the fiber in their garment all the way back to the sheep station where it was grown. Because it's transparent, Baacode allows us to set standards through the supply chain on quality, environmental stewardship, and the treatment of animals and people.

Our internal relationships are also very important to me. Icebreaker's first employees were friends, people I got on well with already. We were all a bit crazy and shared a sense of adventure. I became very conscious of the impact each new person had on the team. New people had to be able to get on with the existing group. We didn't want everyone to be the same, but we wanted a real synergy between people.

We have an incredibly vibrant and fun culture at Icebreaker. It's very creative; there's a strong sense of spirit and purpose. My job is to ensure that we treasure this culture and never take it for granted. It's going to get harder as we grow over time to become a billion-dollar company, but I know it can be done. When I reflect on the role of leadership in emotional bonding, it comes back to one central idea: how can others be allowed to contribute? People give their full commitment to a business only when they feel they're genuinely a part of it.

Awareness: Leadership requires you to be conscious of your impact on other people. In a great book he co-authored called *The Leader's Way*, the Dalai Lama talks about first finding the right view and then finding the right way. An awareness of the right view is critical in business: it's easy to look from one angle, but you need almost a 360-degree view. And then the right way indicates the right thing to do, based on your values, your ethics, and the purpose of the business. At Icebreaker, we have a process that helps us integrate our perspective. When we're creating new products or new systems, we seek out the views of everyone who is affected. The best decisions we make have a complete view of what's going on, and that reveals the right way.

My biggest shift in awareness came when I started seeing Icebreaker as a business model. We call our model Ecosystem, because it balances ecology, economy, and resources. Our objective is profitable sustainability. When you are truly aware, you see that the future has to be based on sustainable enterprises, which is what Icebreaker has been from the beginning.

Doing: Dream and do: that's the right order when it comes to action. It's hard to have a meaningful life if we're just doing. As for dreaming without doing, I don't know anyone who has become successful without purposeful hard work. It's the combination that inspires people and connects them with their dharma, their purpose. I dream of Icebreaker being the global leader in sustainability and the cleanest clothing company in the world. We can demonstrate that it's possible to build a successful business while feeling proud of who you are, what you can contribute, and what the business does.

For me, a dream starts as a possibility. Slowly, the possibility grows and turns into a wave of energy—a feeling of being aligned with the purpose of my life. This takes practice and trust. My intuition hasn't let me down yet. The successful people I know rely on their gut. They analyze the facts, but then they go deep into themselves and wait for the answers to emerge— maybe in the middle of the night, maybe in the shower, maybe when they're playing tennis or drinking wine with friends. That's why it's so important to trust yourself to recognize the feeling deep inside before you leap into action. Doing is based on consciousness.

Empowerment: When you lead a business, empowerment is about allowing the people you work with to find their own power. That's spiritual power, creative power, judgment, mental power, and influence over others. Empowerment motivates others to contribute. They feel valued and realize that they can make a difference. I want others to sense a rising power within themselves. If this power is positive, they will stay loyal to you and the organization. If the power is negative, or is motivated only by money, you will be traded in for a better offer.

Early on, we got the culture right at Icebreaker, so everything has evolved positively. It's a network of authentic relationships. Openness, directness, and honesty create true empowerment within an organization, and then the business will go on to achieve great things. You also have to know when to give up power. To achieve Icebreaker's long-term potential, I've had to shift the power base away from me to my management team. Seven years ago, when I was making this change, I asked a management consultant how he thought I was doing as CEO. He said, "You're not a CEO. You tell people what to do, and you've got all these one-to-one relationships. How can you create a network of relationships within the business so that other people can work out what to do for themselves?"

That was a challenging thing for me to hear, but it was also a turning point. When I first started Icebreaker, I had to do everything myself. It was hard to let go, and the business grew slowly as a result. It took us four years to get to five million dollars in revenues, and I was the constraining force. Two years later Icebreaker was taking in twenty million dollars. What happened in between? I learned how to delegate. I came to see my role as finding the right people and giving them the power to take over the functions I used to think only I could handle. Five years later the business hit over one hundred million dollars, and it's been growing strongly ever since.

Empowering others is a way of saying you trust their judgment and their ability to perform. You are giving them the space to express themselves. Icebreaker is all about our people. As its leader I can't let that slip away. Products come and go, but our company culture must remain strong, healthy, open, honest and energetic if we are going to succeed in the long term.

Responsibility: I used to think that responsibility was a burden. Now I know it's the freedom to choose. When you're running a business, you're making decisions about how to grow that business ethically. That means entering into the unknown, which always carries a degree of risk. There are two types of risk: responsible risk and reckless risk. I'm an entrepreneur. I've always had a sense of adventure. People think I'm a risk taker, but I'm not. The risks I take with Icebreaker have been calculated ones. I've made an assessment, taken the right view, and then acted, knowing that the risks were responsible. For a leader, not taking any risks is abdicating responsibility. But so is failing to let go and assigning others the power to take their own risks.

For me, this has been a maturing process. I take responsibility for our products and our brand, and for making sure we're heading in the right direction. But the business isn't everything. People look and listen to the CEO, so I need to be conscious of my behavior and how it affects others. With that in mind, I take responsibility for my well-being. I have to find the right balance between work, love, and play. If all of us can keep these three areas evolving continually, we'll be leading a rich, harmonious life.

Synchronicity: Entrepreneurs often talk about synchronicity. We share a sense of being in the right place at the right time, but it's more than that. Along the way we've found ourselves looking for something, frustrated by a problem we can't solve, and then a solution suddenly dawns. A chance meeting introduced me to merino wool. That meeting enabled me to connect internationally and to live the kind of life I want to live. A chance meeting, the intention to do something, or the desire to solve a problem—the mysterious way that synchronicity weaves our lives into a pattern is a common theme for people who find a way to be in control of their own destiny.

I feel most "in the zone" when synchronicity is linked with inner purpose: my ability to create intensifies, and so does my ability to inspire others. I'm not always there, but when I am, it feels great. The secret is not to hold on too hard or get too attached to the outcome. Being open to new possibilities makes us feel alive. When we are in touch with our creativity, it's important to listen to how that feels. I believe that synchronicity is generated from that place. Be open to it. Don't be afraid to declare what your soul desires. Attach your intention to it, and be willing to see where it leads. Unless you are connected to a sense of meaning that is totally personal to you, synchronicity can't be really effective. Our ability to engage with our deepest meaning is at the heart of our ability to inspire and lead others. And it's the very core of leadership.

When I was studying marketing at the university, I heard about a philosophy that changed my life: "To get what you want in business, you need to give others what they want." It's a variation on the Golden Rule, an ethical code that can be found in many world cultures: "Treat others as you would have them treat you." To follow this way of thinking, you have to ask yourself a question: what do I want? For me if it was only about the money, forget it. Greed would take over, and I'd be destined to fail. Instead, I wanted the challenge of creating something bigger than myself, something others could contribute to.

How can business be a force for good? We need to challenge the old-school methodology of exploiting resources, the environment, and workers purely for profit. Imagine a society where business leaders are known for their ability to inspire others and create great companies rather than solely for their ability to make money. This is the type of society I want to live in, and this is the new breed of leaders I can see emerging around the world.

Nine

RENATA M. BLACK,
Founding Director of Seven Bar Foundation

Of the leaders who are changing the face of charitable aid around the world, one of the most inspiring is Renata M. Black. She exudes youth and boundless enthusiasm. As a teenager, Renata had an idea to help the poor, and step by step she has carried her dream to the point where she is having a global impact. Her foundation translates profits into microloans, a revolutionary change from the old model of charity as a handout from the rich to the poor. The Seven Bar Foundation, begun by her, is a social enterprise based on her simple observation: that luxury lingerie from Europe was an untapped niche market in the United States. (She likes to say that Seven Bar uses sensuality and seduction to have a social impact.) Through retail outlets and fashion shows, lingerie stamped with the Seven Bar logo is using its success to provide microloans to women around the world.

The hard truth is that there are not enough donor funds in the world to alleviate every preventable problem. The obstacle isn't lack of generosity. In 2010 the United States will give $316 billion to charitable causes. But even this wholehearted generosity has a limit: as soon as you give to one hand that reaches out for aid, another immediately replaces it. Renata asked a breakthrough question: "What if we could take a percentage of that $316 billion and invest it in nonprofit organizations becoming self-sustaining entities?" To her, nonprofits need to work smarter and not harder. The state of the world cannot be left to hope and the unpredictable generosity of donors.

There were specific reasons why Seven Bar targets microloans to women. "I picked women as my vehicle for transformative change," says Renata, "because, to put it simply, they are the root of a society from which all else grows. Children's education, the family environment, health care, population growth—these depend on women and the choices they make. I also feel that women, being nurturers, are more likely than males to spend their profits on their children's well-being. Therefore, when you invest in a woman, you help break the cycle of poverty for the next generation."

Like others who lead from the soul, Renata saw a new trend in the collective consciousness. More consumers are making choices based on their personal values. As she puts it, "Products are no longer objects of necessity—they have become an extension of what we believe in. Research shows that 89 percent of consumers are very likely to switch from one brand to another if the second brand is associated with a good cause. This is even more true of the next generation." Like Jeremy Moon, Renata tells her own remarkable story best.

You can spend years working to reach a defining moment, but there are also moments you don't seek that suddenly decide how you are going to lead the rest of your life. That's what happened to me at fifteen. Nothing was more confusing for me than being a teenager. After my parents died in an airplane crash when I was very small, I was adopted by an aunt and uncle in the United States, where I spent my entire childhood. I never quite knew who I truly was, so I decided to move back to my native Colombia to find my roots. There I could experience the culture, the people, and their passion for life. At fifteen one yearns for that sense of belonging. At the same time I had an abrupt and life-changing encounter with poverty. One day I took the bus to the wrong side of the mountain. I had witnessed poverty in the United States, but what I saw that day in Colombia added a completely new dimension to the experience.

This wrong bus ride was my instant moment of realization: I could have wound up as one of those kids living in a cardboard box. Thousands of them weren't fortunate enough to have the opportunity that had come my way. It was then that my purpose was forever defined. Some of my friends jokingly tell me I have an illness to be so completely obsessed by purpose. I see it a different way: I am fortunate to know exactly why I am on this planet. I feel a larger responsibility that goes beyond one person's purpose. I owe it to my deceased parents to make their lives count. I owe it to my adopted parents for their sacrifice in raising me, and above all I owe it to my people in Colombia, whose existence I can improve. As seen by the rest of the world, getting to live in the United States is like arriving at the top of the mountain. I also see it as an obligation to use the kind of opportunity that Americans take for granted and extend it to parts of the world where there is so much unfulfilled potential.

Before I could turn my teenage ideals into reality, I had to face how enormous poverty is. What could one person possibly do? On the other hand, why would anyone else care about Colombia? I wanted to have a significant lasting impact, so I did what any normal kid would do to get answers. First I went to college. By the time I graduated from the University of North Carolina at Chapel Hill, I had the right skill sets to be materially successful, but that wasn't enough. I couldn't feel successful without giving my life significance. In my next phase I traveled around the world, volunteering in different countries. In Hong Kong I worked with terminally disabled children, in New Zealand with mentally disabled elders, and in India with victims of the tsunami of 2004 who needed to rebuild their villages.

During this last project a desperate woman came up to me and said in Hindi, "I know you have money, but I don't want it. Why don't you teach me how to make money for myself?" A second defining moment had come to me that directed me on my unfolding path. At the time I didn't know how to teach her how to make money, but I set out to find a way.

I had already observed the bad effects of aid sent in from the outside, which served only to make impoverished people more dependent, while doing little to make them self-sufficient. (Over the past thirty years, the most aid-dependent countries have exhibited an average annual growth rate of minus 0.2 percent.) The only way to break this cycle was to offer real opportunity. For example, microfinance involves giving a small loan as seed money to start or grow personal businesses. It's an exit strategy from poverty where the person who receives the loan makes the effort to succeed. Providing this kind of incentive has the opposite effect from simply giving aid.

As my life purpose unveiled itself, I became dedicated to building a social enterprise that provides rungs of opportunity to the poor on a global scale. I am now in the business of providing such ladders to underprivileged women via microfinance. I feel that social enterprises are the future of nonprofits. A social enterprise is different from charity in that it runs like a business and is not reliant on unpredictable generosity. By aligning causes with products, we lead consumers to a feel-good buy. At the same time, we allow nonprofits to have a consistent revenue stream.

Today Lingerie Miami, New York, Los Angeles, and fifteen other cities serve as a high-visibility platform for the Seven Bar Foundation brand. Lingerie Miami was the official launch of the Seven Bar Foundation brand in 2009, generating 170 million media impressions, 120 articles worldwide, and an estimated

$1.7 million in advertising value. In other words, with one event we reached a critical mass in consciousness.

Lingerie New York 2010 will feature the first ever couture line by Atsuko Kudo, whose designs are worn by celebrities like Eva Mendes, Beyoncé, and Lady Gaga. To give buyers the opportunity to purchase products directly from the runway, the foundation is partnering with the latest in technology, Overlay TV. Video from the runway show will be streamed on the most highly visited fashion and media websites, where consumers can click, freeze-frame, and purchase products from any aspect of the show.

As part of our business model for social impact, we have the potential to send our shows around the world, conveying to the next generation our message of sustainable development. The success of the initial shows positioned Seven Bar for its first cause-marketing venture. We partnered with a cosmetics line, Fusion Brands, to do a "Kiss Away Poverty" campaign. A dollar from each sale from their line of lip glosses goes directly to the foundation. In the first three months of the campaign over 100,000 lip glosses were sold, bringing in $100,000 for us. The rise in Fusion Brands' sales has led the campaign to expand globally, sporting the foundation's image and logo on lip gloss packaging and advertising.

The shows are there to inspire people to take two completely opposing concepts like microfinance and lingerie and unite them to become a transformational force. All "Lingerie" brand products and events carry the symbol of a ladder, representing a hand up instead of a handout. My goal is to use the appeal of luxury lingerie to provide exit strategies for underprivileged women around the world far beyond my lifetime. I believe that companies who choose to run their business as "profit with a purpose" will leave more than just products and services behind. They will leave a legacy.

RENATA M. BLACK AND L-E-A-D-E-R-S

Look and Listen: For me, looking and listening is an aspect of receptivity. One of the assets that made me the person I am today is an ability to sense the moods of different people. Receptivity to mood allows you to quickly address or redirect energy according to a person's state. This comes, I think, from a cultural inheritance of mine, which involves showing tact while relying on intuition and awareness of others. Looking in a receptive way also revealed an untapped niche in the fashion market. I tuned in to the trends of a population. Also, I felt that the face of microfinance needed to be more appealing. Visually, the design of the products we brand is seductive and sensual, so the customer sees something that stimulates the purchase and leaves a pleasing impression about supporting a good cause.

Emotional Bonding: Finding an emotional connection drives me every day, and once I make one, I want to maintain it. Emotions are like flowers that need constant nurturing to grow and blossom. However, the way emotions are directed—positively or negatively—is what makes the world turn, markets move, people react, and needs get fulfilled. My own feelings led me to where I am today. I began with a sudden bond to the poor in Colombia. That bond led to the belief that I could make a difference, and belief led to opportunity.

More and more I realize that we invest in people rather than ideas. Every transaction is built on a feeling like trust, hope, exuberance, compassion, and generosity. My foundation is actually in the market of emotions, and it trades in their value. It's our customer's empathy for underprivileged women that fuels a purchase—along with a very different feeling, the sensual feeling of luxury lingerie. It takes the merging of these seemingly opposite feelings, one selfish and the other selfless, to create our brand.

We are building customer loyalty through another emotional bond, which stimulates a sense of power in the customer, the power that comes from knowing that your purchase supports your values and a desire to make a difference in the world. *Doing good at the point of sale:* I believe that this is the future of commerce and will lead to meaningful change on the planet.

But the deepest emotions go far beyond this. In developing countries people living in poverty lack funds but have very strong value systems. They are huge believers in God. In the field the loans lent to women create a bond of loyalty. It is their integrity that has produced a 98 percent repayment rate globally. In our office, from the interns to the managers, a shared dedication and passion is our bond. Seven Bar is a daily choreography of emotions in support of one guiding vision.

Awareness: The key to my leadership role is being aware of myself, and of where I come from. Of course, circumstances along the way have shaped me and helped manifest my destiny. None of that would have happened, however, without my being keenly aware that I could easily be among the 60 percent of the world's population who subsist on less than two dollars a day.

Another important aspect of my self-awareness is purpose. The trail to success is littered with frustration and setbacks, and you must make sacrifices all the time on behalf of your mission. I've been fortunate in having a sense of purpose since I was very young, long before I founded the Seven Bar Foundation. My purpose had three parts: to live life at the fullest, to be the best I could be, and to leave the world a better place because I had lived in it. These three things define my self-awareness and drive me every day.

I also have to be aware of the situation around me and how it is changing. A turning point came when I noticed that people were ready to take on more purchasing power, not in terms of money but in terms of making a difference. So their desire for more meaning matched my self-awareness, which has always been based on meaning. The two came together naturally, which is a crucial element in all success stories.

Doing: I look back and realize that I am the quintessential doer. My innate hunger drives my action. It's in my DNA to take initiative, finding undiscovered paths and innovative solutions. I live by the idea that you are the architect of your own life. The amount of time and dedication that are required to get to my goal have never been an obstacle. However, I also realize that every path has redirected me to other paths; at times mine has been a winding road.

The path you walk is the one you have paved. Doing entails leading by example. If I am going to be fueling businesses by impoverished women so that they can become sustainable, mine must be a sustainable business, too. Finally, I have learned to work smarter, not harder. This implies a level of awareness that must exist before action is undertaken. As much as possible, I want my actions to seamlessly tie over to other goals. With this strategy in mind, my day is incredibly active but coherent and smooth at the same time.

Empowerment: As you know by now, my goal is empowerment first and foremost. I can trace this back to an early age, when the rules imposed by teachers and parents seemed impossible to challenge. As a result, I felt repressed for most of my childhood, and I found relief by rebelling. I never thought of changing the rules because that simply wasn't an option—the social systems were set in stone.

I remember when I first saw the light through the cracks. I was volunteering for a nonprofit in India when I approached the head of the organization with an idea about microfinancing for women. I did a full-on presentation that lasted nearly three hours, after which he patted me on the back and said, "Do it." That was my first empowering moment. I was encouraged to make something happen. I was in such utter shock that I exploded with passion and dedication like a pressure cooker! One never forgets what it feels like to own one's own power, a life-changing feeling that I want to give women everywhere. On that day I realized that I could be a force for change without boundaries.

Responsibility: I'm very attracted to the notion that responsibility is the ability to respond. Some people are born with this ability; others have it thrust upon them. I responded to my circumstance by creating a model for sustainable change. I am a great believer in responding to your circumstance in a meaningful way. So from a very young age I've carried with me a sense that I am deeply responsible to my Colombian people, my deceased parents, and my adopted family.

Everyone is born into what I call their original responsibility. Then, if you accept a leadership role, you gain a new level of responsibility, this time to your employees and to the trust being placed in you financially. The more responsible I am, the more phenomenal are the people surrounding me. I feel responsible every day for leading them on the path of growth. Yet always there is a responsibility to myself to make it count. If I were a sailboat, emotional bonding would be my boat, empowerment would be my sail, and responsibility would be my rudder.

Synchronicity: I thrive on unknown possibilities. I live very much by the motto of Buckminster Fuller: "If you want to change something, build a new model that makes the existing model obsolete." As a pioneer, you experience a roller coaster of emotions. For years you wake up every day obsessed by an idea that many do not understand. You look ahead and tell yourself, "This isn't the straightest way to get there. But is there a bend in the road for a reason?" As you tango with destiny to arrive at your goal, a sequence of almost magical events occurs. Then you sigh, "Okay, this is definitely the right path."

More and more awareness fine-tunes your efforts until you get to the ultimate awareness, which defines your ultimate success. My big lesson recently has been, "You can do anything but not everything." I know I am great at certain parts of my business, but I fall short in others. My weaknesses were holding me back from reaching my maximum potential.

At the exact moment that I realized this, I came across an empowered woman who would become my future partner. Kim Hoedeman and I exactly complement each other. We both found ourselves at a crossroads. We wanted to be redefined, and by supporting each other, we have manifested our mutual destiny. Although we zoom through fifteen-hour workdays, we still pause and look back to this intersection as the strongest synchronistic moment in each of our lives. Together we are an unbeatable force.

Renata M. Black has become the unstoppable force she describes. Although she speaks of having drive and dedication in her DNA, she also describes having walked a path. Every step of the path involved deeper awareness. She discovered her life's passion while discovering who she was. The two have merged, which is the purpose of leading from the soul. As she says, awareness fine-tunes your path until you reach your ultimate goal.

The critical moment was when I received permission from my superior in India to "do it." This moment set the precedent for my life today. There were possibilities within me that I would never have guessed in a million years. The beginning was barely a glimpse of light through the cracks of the system, but the effect has been huge, and I intend to pass it on for the rest of my life.

PART THREE

TEN PRINCIPLES OF LEADERSHIP

Ten

A TEMPLATE FOR AWARENESS

I have done my best in these pages to make this book rich in meaning. As a result, what is a slender volume is still packed with ideas, exercises, and suggestions. It's a lot to absorb. But the basic message is simple. We all have a still place inside us that is the source of everything that gives our lives meaning. This is the soul, and it is the place great leaders turn to for their inspiration, and for the answers to all their important questions.

How will you know that you are drawing from the soul's unique perspective? We have looked at a number of ways to know that you are being true to the highest calling of spirit, so let me close this book by pulling together ten basic principles that function as a template for awareness, which is the wellspring of the universe. When you recognize these principles in action, you will know that you are truly on the soul's path.

1. Leaders and followers co-create each other. Followers express a need, and the leader supplies a response. Both arise together. When they don't, there is a leadership vacuum; at such times, needs become more intense and

eventually desperate, paving the way for exploitation and dictatorship.

2. Just as individuals grow from the inside out, so do groups. The group's needs must be met wherever they are. Sometimes a group needs a parent or protector, at other times a motivator, healer, or spiritual guide. Needs fuel change. The leader operates from the soul level to cause inner change, which then gets expressed on the surface as success.

3. The outcome of any situation is defined in advance by the vision that goes into solving it. Therefore inner qualities determine results.

4. The responses shared by leaders and followers are built into us, guiding us to evolve and progress. The soul is aware of how to unfold our evolution to produce the highest and best outcome in any situation.

5. Needs are designed to evolve, and a leader must be aware of this in order to foresee the future of the group and anticipate its needs. In rising order the group's needs are for safety and security, achievement, cooperation, understanding, creativity, moral values, and spiritual fulfillment. All these are inner and outer needs that have evolved over time in the life of every society.

6. For every need, a leader must play the right role. The need for security calls for a protector; achievement calls for a motivator; cooperation calls for a team builder; understanding calls for a nurturer; creativity calls for an innovator; moral values call for a transformer; spiritual fulfillment calls for a sage, or seer. This matchup is organic—the soul knows how to fulfill any need with the least effort and

struggle. A leader who can tap directly into this knowledge gains tremendous power for good, far beyond that of someone who concentrates only on external goals and rewards.

7. The leader who understands the hierarchy of needs and responses will succeed; the leader who aims only for external goals (money, victory, power) will falter in the area that counts most: guiding the evolution of his followers.

8. By ascending the hierarchy of needs, any group can be made to feel inspired and unified. Great leaders are in touch with every level of human experience. They understand that their followers yearn for freedom, love, and spiritual worth; therefore they are not afraid to hold out higher goals that lie beyond mere material rewards. But at the same time they don't lead from the mountaintop. Every leader is also everyman. A lower need like the need to feel safe must be understood, genuinely felt, and then fully met before moving to a higher need. The challenge at hand can be as seemingly small as a guided discussion in which people feel safe to express their innermost feelings or as profound as leading a society out of oppression. The soul knows every level of life; a great leader aspires to know the same.

9. Leading from the soul means giving of yourself. It means you supply trust, stability, compassion, and hope. You spend time investing in relationships with those who turn to you for answers. Unafraid of forming emotional bonds, you don't hide from any need as it unfolds. By contrast, leaders who are led astray by the desire to protect themselves emotionally, who limit their responses, or who

cling to their egos, wind up being failures. They may have success in material terms, but if they do, it will be devoid of inner worth.

10. The soul brings order out of disorder. It brings creative leaps, unexpected answers, and synchronicities that are like gifts from the heart of mystery. No matter how complex and confusing a situation looks, leadership is possible when you are comfortable with uncertainty. Once they see the hidden spiritual order that lies beneath what seems to be chaos, inspired leaders thrive on uncertainty. You must learn how to manage the fact that situations are tangled, otherwise the group you lead will be crippled by turmoil. There is always a jumble of needs and responses that must be sorted out. Fear and survival, competition and creativity, beliefs and personalities make their demands. They each have a voice, whether we hear them or not, but underneath the jumbled surface there is only one voice, the silent whisper of spirit, which understands everything.

Think of these ten principles as a template for awareness. Ideally, you would apply it to everything you do. All models of leadership give much the same general advice when it comes to managing tasks and motivating other people. But they leave out the most important thing: a basis in Being. Being is the ground of everything. It is pure awareness, the womb of creativity, the generator of evolution. When the final story is told, leadership is the most crucial choice one can make—the decision to be. Only someone who turns for wisdom to the silent domain of the soul can thrive in the midst of chaos. Such a person will be remembered as a great leader. Yet being is everyone's birthright; awareness is built into our brains as well as our spirit. There is always a new phase of evolution, and evolution is guided by need.

The world's wisdom traditions define truth as a single spark that burns down the whole forest. If a leader is willing to be that spark, others will see the truth within him. Craving direction and the fulfillment of their needs, they will value what he offers, which is the first step toward valuing it in themselves. As a leader, you may find occasion to tell your followers why you wanted to raise them to a higher level, but in your heart you will know that you did it for yourself. To walk your own path is enough.

Acknowledgments

This book was inspired by a course I teach at the Kellogg Graduate School of Management, Northwestern University. I'd like to thank the school's former dean, Dipak Jain, for encouraging me to start the course and for his continual support during the past eight years. My teaching colleague, Michelle Buck, deserves appreciation for her expertise and inspiration—she has awakened many CEOs and other top executives to their own personal journeys.

Two corporate visionaries have invited the soul of leadership into their daily operations: Al Carey of Frito-Lay and George Zimmer and the board at Men's Wearhouse. It's exciting to see them in the forefront of change, and the same goes for Jeremy Moon and Renata M. Black, who generously provided me with their personal stories. Thanks to all.

I have been proudly associated as a senior scientist with the Gallup Organization, which has collected more data on leadership and the workplace than any other source in the world. Thanks to Gallup's CEO, Jim Clifton, for giving me this privilege. I'm also grateful to Danielle Posa, my liaison at Gallup, who generously provides me with any information I need.

Gallup is the source of two groundbreaking books that

guided me through many issues: *Strengths-Based Leadership* by Tom Rath and Barry Conchie, and *Well-Being: The Five Essential Elements* by Tom Rath and Jim Harter. I cannot recommend them highly enough to anyone who wants a positive approach to leadership based on results gleaned from thousands of interviews.

My longtime friend and wise editor, Peter Guzzardi, deserves much thanks for his patience in bringing this book to fruition. He manages to make rewrites easy when no one else could. At the publishers I have had the loyalty and support of some wonderful people, including Shaye Areheart, Jenny Frost, Tina Constable, and Julia Pastore. Our warm relationship has been the mainstay of my writing career. It has now extended to include Maya Mavjee, who has welcomed me to a new phase of our partnership.

The Chopra Center includes the most faithful support group anyone could wish for: Carolyn and Felicia Rangel and Tori Bruce, my heartfelt thanks.

And as always, unending love to my wife, Rita, and our children, Mallika, Gotham, Sumant, and Candice, and to my beautiful babies Tara, Leela, and Krishan: home for me is wherever you are.

About the Author

DEEPAK CHOPRA is the author of more than fifty-five books translated into over thirty-five languages, including numerous *New York Times* bestsellers in both fiction and nonfiction.

Also available from Deepak Chopra

The Book of Secrets

Who am I? Where did I come from? Why am I here?

The Book of Secrets, by the internationally bestselling author, Deepak Chopra, focuses on the universal questions: who we really are, and why we are here.

Crafted with all the skills that have made his previous books bestsellers, *The Book of Secrets* will be essential reading for Deepak Chopra's huge number of followers worldwide, and also appeal to everyone searching for the meaning of life, and looking for answers to the questions: Who Am I? Where Did I Come From? and Why Am I Here?

Each of the fifteen chapters discusses a 'secret' - such as: The world is in you; Transformation is not the same as change; Death is conquered by dying every day; Everything is pure essence. Chopra believes that 'Every life is a book of secrets ready to be opened', and that the only way to discover the answers to these secrets is to delve inside yourself, and cease to be a mystery to yourself. Only by going to 'the still point inside' can you see life as it really is.

£11.99   ISBN 9781844135554

Order direct from www.riderbooks.co.uk

Also available from Deepak Chopra

The Ultimate Happiness Prescription: 7 Keys to Joy and Enlightenment

The perfect antidote to deep recession: how to experience joy

In *The Ultimate Happiness Prescription*, bestselling author Deepak Chopra shows how to experience joy in spite of living in difficult or trying times.

By looking through the lens of our contemporary understanding of consciousness, combined with Eastern philosophy, he has created a set of principles for living with ease. The result is an inspiring and instructive journey that leads to a prescription for living life mindfully, with a light heart and with effortless spontaneity – a prescription only Dr Deepak Chopra could write.

With words like 'depression' and 'recession' in the air, he underlines the importance of keeping an eye on the positive aspects of life and finding ways to experience joy no matter what is happening to you. This remarkably clear and helpful book explains how to maintain an optimistic outlook and experience the benefits of having a happy heart and soul, no matter what the circumstances.

£8.99   ISBN 9781846042379

Order direct from www.riderbooks.co.uk